Oscar Kosarin is an associate professor of music theater at the College-Conservatory of Music, University of Cincinnati, Ohio. He is a self-taught musician who, as a pianist, performed at such nightclubs as the Stork Club, El Morocco, and the Copacabana. Mr. Kosarin's Broadway experience has been in the roles of conductor, arranger, vocal coach, and pianist. He also composed the musical score for the documentary film *Virginia—A Pursuit of Happiness,* which won first prize at the Virgin Islands Film Festival in 1976.

Dedicated to my students, who constantly challenged and inspired me to find new ways of opening the doors to their own talents.

Oscar Kosarin

THE SINGING ACTOR

How to Be a Success in Musical Theater and Nightclubs

A SPECTRUM BOOK

Prentice-Hall, Inc., Englewood Cliffs, New Jersey 07632

iii

Library of Congress Cataloging in Publication Data

Kosarin, Oscar.
  The singing actor.

  "A Spectrum Book."
  Bibliography: p.
  Includes index.
  1. Singing—Instruction and study. 2. Acting—Study and teaching.
3. Music—Vocational guidance. 4. Acting—Vocational guidance.
MT820.K83 1983   784.9'34   83-4535
ISBN 0-13-810978-8
ISBN 0-13-810960-5 (pbk.)

This book is available at a special discount when ordered
in bulk quantities. Contact Prentice-Hall, Inc., General
Publishing Division, Special Sales, Englewood Cliffs, N. J. 07632.

© 1983 by Prentice-Hall, Inc., Englewood Cliffs, New Jersey 07632

A SPECTRUM BOOK

10 9 8 7 6 5 4 3 2 1

Printed in the United States of America

Manufacturing buyer: Doreen Cavallo
Cover design by Hal Siegel

ISBN 0-13-810978-8

ISBN 0-13-810960-5 {PBK.}

Prentice-Hall International, Inc., *London*
Prentice-Hall of Australia Pty. Limited, *Sydney*
Prentice-Hall Canada Inc., *Toronto*
Prentice-Hall of India Private Limited, *New Delhi*
Prentice-Hall of Japan, Inc., *Tokyo*
Prentice-Hall of Southeast Asia Pte. Ltd., *Singapore*
Whitehall Books Limited, *Wellington, New Zealand*
Editora Prentice-Hall do Brasil Ltda., *Rio de Janeiro*

iv

Contents

II
VOICE AND DICTION

III
THE BODY AND MOVEMENT

IV
NIGHTCLUBS

APPENDIXES

Foreword

The following pages are unique and remarkable. Oscar Kosarin has placed all singers in a single category and has wisely pointed out the problems that all of them experience, whether they sing in an opera house or a nightclub.

Not content with spelling out the problems, Kosarin has analyzed and examined each of them in such a way that the course to resolving them becomes a logical, inevitable next step.

The Singing Actor deals not only with the means by which a song can become a drama, but provides unusual physical exercises that the performer will find invaluable. Kosarin deals clearly with such diverse and essential subjects as lyric analysis, emotional projection, diction, bodily movement, breathing, relaxation, and many others. The methods of dealing with each of these various components are clearly defined.

No other single book within my own experience projects so many ways of resolving the multiple problems all singers encounter. One remarkable aspect of this book is that Oscar Kosarin has managed to clarify difficult problems in copious detail and suggests such simple, clear methods of disposing of them that it seems hard to believe that no other writer on this general subject has tackled both the problems and the resolutions before.

The first stumbling block for many singing actors is their inability to recognize consciously what they need to accomplish if they want to satisfy themselves as well as their audiences. Many are unaware of the fact that they are dealing with a mode of expression that involves a *craft*. Until this one simple if profound aspect of true artistry is recognized, little can be done to correct faults and gain insights into organized methods of expression. Too many singing actors begin with *feeling,* which is in truth the end product. Attaining the ability to communicate feeling is not, in itself, a simple matter.

The Singing Actor provides the step-by-step approach to achieving and maintaining a high level of acting–singing performance. It is presented in a clear, concise manner, and the performer of all ages and levels of experience will find it invaluable.

Lehman Engel

Preface

This book attempts to guide the professional singing actor in performance techniques for the musical theater stage, nightclubs, and other musical media. I also believe that the serious student and amateur will benefit from the material discussed here. I stress the word *serious*. Too often the musical theater stage is treated with disrespect. Many people believe that success in this field depends solely on having an unusual personality or on the whims of chance. On the contrary, the demands placed on the performer in today's theatrical profession are great indeed and constantly being extended.

The singer auditioning today for a Broadway show or a reputable summer stock company is expected not only to sing well. He must also move like a dancer and be able to perform the most difficult choreographic routines. He must have a pleasing stage personality, be a convincing actor, and be able to speak English without a regional accent. Finally, he must have the flexibility to be able to adapt himself to a great variety of performance styles.

Consider the following Broadway musicals and films that have appeared during the past years. The first three have had recent revivals.

My Fair Lady
West Side Story
Hair
Pippin
A Chorus Line
The Wiz
Ain't Misbehavin'
Shenandoah
42nd Street
All That Jazz

Each of these shows is written in a specific musical idiom having a particular feel and color. The styles vary from conventional music based on European traditions, to jazz, rock, country-western and all kinds of improbable combinations of any of these.

Now notice the following list of star performers who have appeared in musicals or musical films:

Rex Harrison
Angela Lansbury
Glynis Johns
Ben Vereen
Gwen Verdon
Frank Sinatra
John Denver
Kris Kristofferson
Joel Grey
Liza Minnelli
Barbra Streisand

Again, a great variety of backgrounds is apparent, together with individual strengths and weaknesses. The first three performers on the list each have had long careers as straight actors in plays and films. Although Rex Harrison and Glynis Johns barely get by as singers, Angela Lansbury is both an outstanding singer *and* dancer. Ben Vereen and Gwen Verdon were featured dancers at the start of their careers and later developed their singing and acting skills. Frank Sinatra's career led him from big band singer to straight actor Denver and Kristofferson made their mark as recording stars before becoming actors in films. Joel Grey's career began in the Borscht Circuit as a comedian and M.C. Minnelli and Streisand, on the other hand, had starring roles in musicals early in their careers and then went into films.

Given the great variety of musical and dramatic styles that are to be found in the American musical theater and in American popular music and the diversified backgrounds of the performers who have achieved reputations in these fields, by what criteria can young performers be guided in order to acquire the kind of education that will prepare them for their profession? Are there any common threads that run through all superior performances, regardless of style or genre? Can any meaningful comparisons be made between rock singing and legitimate singing; between musical comedy and opera? What do Renata Scotto and Barbra Streisand have in common? James Taylor and Luciano Pavarotti?

It is my contention that there *is* a commonality linking these divergent performance styles, that certain universal qualities are present in all superior performances, as follows:

1. A consistently high level of energy is maintained. Energy is most often associated with strength or liveliness. However, these are the more obvious manifestations. The good performer can whisper or be silent; he can stand stock still and yet be brimming with energy. His power comes from inner intensity and concentration.
2. There is a personal involvement with the text of the song. The performer can let go of himself so that he seems to actually experience the thoughts and feelings that the lyric expresses.
3. A heightened sense of "reality" is evoked. The performer presents a carefully selected portion of "reality," rejects all unessential elements, and brings to the audience only that which is relevant and interesting.
4. A strong sense of audience communication is established. The performer is able to share his skills and talents with the audience and sensitively responds to the feedback that he receives from the audience.
5. The performer is perceived to be a unique individual. He has the courage to show his true personality, thereby revealing the qualities that make him different.

Look at the preceding qualifications and take note of the words *high* level of energy, *personal* involvement, *heightened* sense of reality, and *strong* feeling of communication. These words make crucial comments about performance in general. They indicate that what is demanded of the performer is a condensation of experience so that matters of great meaning and consequence can be expressed within a short time span and in a unique way. Thus, in the course of a single refrain of a song, the singer may experience events and feelings that in real life might span weeks, months, or years.

Another reason why so much intensification is required of the performer relates to the subject matter of most song and drama; this most often has to do with winning or losing at love, with strong conflicts and critical points in the lives of people. Most of these experiences are once-in-a-lifetime happenings and cannot be treated lightly. The performer must use the total range of his talents to make them believable.

In view of the multiplicity of skills required in musical theater and the allied fields of popular music and films, how does the student or young professional go about acquiring the training necessary for such a career? To be sure, there are universities, conservatories, and professional schools that offer programs in the performing arts. However, although there are a number of excellent schools from which to choose, none that I know of has a faculty that is of consistently high quality in *all* performance areas. The usual route is for the student to attempt to gain entrance into a school that stresses his particular field of interest, say, singing, and then hope to catch up on the skills of dancing and acting later on. As a result, the most meaningful training, that of consolidating skills, will often not begin until the student has graduated from school and has settled in one of the large metropolises where the best teachers are to be found.

Unfortunately, the student performer cannot get his education in the structured way that, for instance, a law or business student can. By necessity, he must pick up his skills in bits and pieces as opportunities present themselves, and it is not unusual for this process to continue throughout a career.

Aside from formal training, the best school is the experience of performing in public. The performer knows really nothing of himself until he is tested before a live audience. More than any teacher, the audience will tell him whether he is being true or false, dull or funny, communicative or narcissistic. Through trial and error he will correct his mistakes, discovering what works and what doesn't. If he learns to listen to the audience, it will teach him about timing and how to adjust his tempo to its mood. When the performer also has the opportunity of working under a talented stage director, choreographer, or musical director, or with performers who are more advanced than he is, learning obviously increases enormously.

Although nightclubs and pop concerts, as opposed to musical theater, hardly offer the performer any directional guidance, they can still provide valuable lessons. The unpredictable audiences and the noise and distractions that are typical of this environment test the performer's concentration and ability to project his personality under adverse circumstances. Furthermore, without a script to work from and only himself to rely on, he learns, within the small confines of a nightclub or pop concert stage, to create his personal drama.

An overall view of the learning opportunities available to the young performer reveals that his education in many cases is incomplete, discontinuous, and haphazard. Consequently, a far greater responsibility for self-development falls on his shoulders than it does to other professionals.

To make the most of his opportunities, he must know his strengths and weaknesses, have enough self-reliance to acknowledge the gaps in his education, and fill them in with supplementary study. He must continually educate himself by reading, watching other performers, observing daily life, sharing with peers his questions and doubts, becoming more sensitive to both the objective world around him and the subjective world within him. He must be able to develop the powers of his imagination so that he can extend the boundaries of his own limited existence and incorporate within himself the lives and experiences of countless other individuals. He must cultivate the spontaneity that may have become diminished in the process of bending to life's necessities.

The challenges for the performer are formidable; the rewards are uncertain. The only justification for pursuing such a career is an overwhelming need to perform, an unquenchable determination, and an equally great love for the art.

Given the difficulties that the profession offers, it would be presumptuous for the author to claim to provide solutions to the endless problems that the performer will encounter. The aim of this book is rather to activate the performer's imagination and to explore with him the dimly seen path of his potential.

The emphasis throughout the book will be on the practical elements of performing rather than on theoretical formulations or abstract concepts. Some of the suggestions are purely common sense; others are innovative—

a reflection of the author's background as a teacher at the College-Conservatory of Music, University of Cincinnati and a longtime conductor, vocal coach, and arranger on Broadway.

The general plan is to separate the components of a song and examine each element in detail. Through numerous examples and exercises, the reader will become exposed to the many possibilities of individual interpretation that are contained in the seeds of the lyrics and the melody of a song. Following this, the process of reconnecting the elements into a single whole, or gestalt, takes place. Here the most important unifier is that of character, in the theatrical sense. The reader is urged to ask himself the questions: Who sings the song? What has happened to him? What emotions drive him at the moment? and so on. The answers to these questions will fit the various elements together so that coherence results.

One further comment: Although the book proceeds in a structured manner, covering what seems to the author a logical progression of study, it may also be used as a working manual. When specific problems need to be solved, a reference to the particular chapter will prove helpful.

ACKNOWLEDGMENTS

Grateful acknowledgment is made to the late Lehman Engel for his unfailing support and critical advice; to Richard Vance, who first suggested the writing of this book; and to Jack Watson for his valuable suggestions.

THE SONG
AS DRAMA

I

The Song as Drama

1

If we accept a simple definition of acting as the portrayal on the stage of some part of the human experience that is shared with an audience, then, in a sense, every singer is also an actor. If, with equal simplicity, we define drama as a prose or verse composition written for performance by actors, then every song can be taken to be a drama. The central figure of this drama is the singing actor.

Not all singers, however, are singing actors, nor do all want to be. There are many singers, especially in the field of personal appearances, who are content to be primarily entertainers and display their special qualities of voice and the congeniality of their personality. With such performers—and this is not intended as a disparagement—the song becomes secondary. It becomes a vehicle through which the above mentioned aims are effected.

Although he can also be an entertainer, when he so chooses, the singing actor by distinction gives primacy to the song, especially to the text of the song. He views himself as a character in a play; the song is the play. The singing actor accordingly transforms himself in response to the role he has accepted, and he does this in his own particular way. He adapts his personality so that it is consistent with the content and character of the song. He minimizes personal affectations and idiosyncracies and stresses rather the truth of expression that the song evokes in him.

There are two basic performance contexts in which the singing actor performs. The first and most obvious is opera and musical theater. Here, as in any play, the performer becomes a character. He is given a script that provides a story line, defines what kind of person he is, and what relationships he has with the other characters in the play. When a song emerges in the course of the plot, it may fulfill one of the following functions:

- It may further the plot; new information is disclosed by the lyrics.
- The song may reflect the mood or atmosphere of the scene and thus intensify it.
- It may clarify our understanding of a character's motives and attitudes.
- It may presage what is to happen after the song is ended.

A song in a musical play may be designed to fulfill one or more of these functions. "Bali Ha'i" from *South Pacific* is an example of a song that fulfills several of them. In it, Bloody Mary entices Lieutenant Cable to go to the island, Bali Ha'i, in order that he meet and possibly marry her daughter, Liat. When the song is ended, we have learned something of Bloody Mary's philosophy of life and of her intentions regarding Cable and her daughter. By describing the island in alluring terms, she excites his curiosity. Finally, the song points ahead at what is to come, and the audience understands that Cable has been ensnared and will go to the island.

Not all songs in musical theater are as integrated into the script as this. At times the purpose of a musical number is to break up the continuity of the plot and to provide an interval of pure musical entertainment. The musicals of the 1920s and 1930s were generally of this kind, since their plots were usually farcical with the accent on comedy. However, the use of musical interludes solely for entertainment purposes is still an important part of musical theater. "Hello Dolly," the title song from the show, is a good example of such a number. Its function is to provide an opportunity for a full-blown lavish production number, employing masses of singers and dancers to dazzle the audience. And it does just that; it is one of the greatest show-stoppers in all musicals.

The second basic performance context that the singing actor encounters is so far removed from the first that there may seem to be hardly a connection between the two. We speak now of nightclubs, cafés, variety shows, personal appearances, and social occasions where live entertainment is provided. In contrast to the first situation, the performer here is completely free to choose his material and to express himself in any manner that suits him. This freedom, nevertheless, is not without consequences. It imposes a responsibility on the performer that may not be entirely welcome, for now he must make a number of important decisions regarding repertoire, style of delivery, interpretation, musical arrangements, costumes, and a host of other details. He becomes, in essence, his own producer, writer, and director. Perhaps as important as any of the previously named elements, there is the question of whether to present oneself as an entertainer or as a singing actor. This book is obviously oriented to guide those who make the latter choice.

For the singing actor performing in a nightclub or similar medium, the idea of song as drama becomes a useful tool with which to create a specific environment for each song. It gives him the means of expanding his imaginative powers and greatly increases the number of interpretive choices open to him.

By accepting the premise that a song in itself is not only a miniature scene, but that the scene can be imagined to be part of a larger drama, the singer acts, in effect, *as if* the song emerged from a musical play. This technique of expanding a song into a drama will be more fully developed later in the chapter on nightclubs.

For now we will analyze the separate components of song in a systematic way, so that each can be given detailed attention. The performer may find the practicing of one element of a song at a time—for instance, reciting a lyric, rather than singing it—to be either frustrating or exciting, depending on his attitude. Obviously, if his approach is one of willingness to delve into new territories and test the effectiveness of the suggested exercises, the benefits for him will be proportionately greater. It is important to keep in mind that the final goal of analysis is synthesis, the putting back together of the pieces in such a skillful way that no seams show. The audience must never see the technique that he has worked on so diligently. All that should be seen and heard is a performance that has the quality of effortlessness and spontaneity.

Lyric
Analysis

2

Central to drama is the script or text where the events that occur in the play are described, its characters delineated, and the relationships between characters revealed. It is the actor's task to breathe life into the written words. He does this first by understanding the meaning of the words—a primarily intellectual study. He then probes into his particular character; he searches for identity and motivation. In the course of his search, personal fragments of his life, memories, associations, cherished beliefs, and values may surface, and a process of amalgamation takes place, resulting in a blending of the "real" and the pretended.

Similarly, in song, all the material that is necessary for the creation of a performance resides in the lyric. This corresponds to the script of the play. The lyric is the source from which all the choices of interpretation will be made, and it is our first order of study.

A lyric can originate in various ways: It may be an existing poem that a composer finds suitable as a text for a song—the great bulk of the classical song literature has originated in this manner. Or a lyric may be set to a previously written melody. In musical theater and pop music, either starting point has been used. The songs of Richard Rodgers are interesting in this respect. When he collaborated earlier in his career with Lorenz Hart, Rodgers customarily originated a melodic idea to which Hart would fit a lyric. With Oscar Hammerstein, the process was usually reversed, the lyric preceding the music.

Whatever the sequence of collaboration, a strong chemistry is at work when words and music are combined. A haunting melodic line may make prosaic words seem to say more than they actually do, and a striking word picture can enhance a commonplace melody. When both words and music are of high quality and are skillfully joined so that one supports the other, the song is far greater than the sum of its parts.

The effect of mutual reinforcement comes partly from the fact that words shaped in a certain way are "musical." The sound sequences of "Oh What a Beautiful Mornin' "—the rhythms created by the alternation of vowels and consonants, stressed and unstressed syllables—cannot be called anything but musical, and the sensitive composer will utilize and enhance these elements when giving the lyric a setting. Aside from musical values, the power of both words and music to evoke emotion and to create moods is another reason for the ability of songs to affect us so keenly.

Although words and music are inseparable in the performance of a song, we will begin our study with the analysis of lyrics. The reason for this is primarily that words are more concrete in their meaning than melody. Being representatives of things and ideas, words are more accessible to interpretation, and although both elements have emotional content, that of lyrics is far less ambiguous than that of melody. The following example will illustrate:

> Don't know why there's no sun up in the sky,
> Stormy weather.[1]

These words express feelings that are unmistakably sad. The associations that come to mind are gloomy days and depressing events. A melody that accompanies the above words follows on page 8:

Don't know   why_____   there's no   sun up   in   the sky, Storm-y   Weath-er,___

If you had never heard the words to this melody, could you interpret them as cheerful, even jaunty? Just for fun, imagine these three bars of music coupled with the following words:

> Don't know why
> I've been feeling awf'lly spry,
> Must be lo-ove.

The intent here is not to satirize or downgrade Harold Arlen's remarkable melody, but to point out the natural ambiguity of music and the difficulty of pinning specific emotions to a series of notes alone.

Beyond this, a strong reason for beginning the analysis of songs with words rather than music is the power of words to activate images that, in turn, bring about physical and emotional changes in the body. This chain reaction of responses can be brought to awareness and under the control of the performer.

VOCABULARY

The first and most obvious consideration in understanding a lyric is the literal meaning of words. Although this seems self-evident, singers often sing words that they do not know the meaning of. The fault usually stems from the habit of mechanically memorizing lyrics until they become automatically ingrained in the mind. Without thought, musical phrases become dull and lifeless. For instance, how many female singers have sung "I'm bromidic"/"Wonderful Guy" from *South Pacific* by faking the meaning of the word? It usually is performed as if the word were something complimentary, rather than its actual meaning of platitudinous and unoriginal.

When Carrie in *Carousel* sings

> When we work in the mill, weavin' at the loom,
> Y'gaze absentminded at the roof,
> And half the time the shuttle gets twisted in the threads
> 'Till y'can't tell the warp from the woof.[2]

---

[2]"Mister Snow," by Richard Rodgers and Oscar Hammerstein II. Copyright ©1945 by Williamson Music, Inc. Copyright renewed. Sole selling agent: T.B. Harms Company (c/o

8

Most anyone can guess that *warp* and *woof* have something to do with weaving, but what, specifically, do these words mean? A clear mental image will register in the eyes and on the face; a fuzzy one will mirror itself correspondingly.

> If I invite
> A boy some night
> To dine on my fine
> Finnan haddie...[3]

Not to know what *finnan haddie* means is to miss a very funny joke.

In *Kiss Me Kate,* Cole Porter tosses around a variety of geographical references: The *Jungfrau* is a mountain peak in Switzerland; *Firenze* is the Italian name for the city of Florence; *Duomo, Ponte Vecchio,* and *Pitti Palace* are all landmarks in Florence.

That the majority of the audience will find these names unfamiliar is irrelevant. It is the performer's job, by means of expressiveness, to make the audience understand. The audience will *see* the meaning in the eyes and face and body language of the performer and will hear it in his vocal inflections. If, however, the performer does not understand the lyrics, the audience will see only a blank face.

PUNCTUATION

The purpose of punctuation is to separate sentences into groups of related words and to indicate the degree of relatedness between the various parts. Punctuation marks notify the reader (performer) that a short pause is to be made in order to distinguish one thought from another.

The musical counterpart to punctuation is called *phrasing.* A phrase is a musical thought, corresponding to a sentence or clause. In classical music it is indicated by means of a long curved line written over the notes that comprise the phrase. The end of a phrase is often characterized by a pause (rest) or a long note.

When there is a perfect blending of words and music, as in many of the songs of Rodgers and Hammerstein, punctuation and musical phrasing are in synchrony, and every comma, semicolon, and period is matched by an analogous pause in the music. This makes it easy for the singer, since the punctuation is built into the musical phrasing. However, such absolute synchrony of words and music happens relatively rarely. In many instances, it is not even desired by the composer and lyricist. The juxtaposition of words and music often produces interplays and momentary conflicts that can be delightfully exciting. In such cases, the observance of punctuation—and consequently of clarity of meaning of a lyric—can be problematic.

For instance, in order to achieve effects of agitation or excitement, a composer will sometimes crowd together a series of notes without a pause. If the tempo is rapid, it may be difficult for the singer to observe the commas, colons, question marks, and so forth. Yet they must be observed for the sake of clarity. For example:

> From all I've read, alone in bed,
> From A to Zed about 'em,
> Since love is blind, then from the mind,
> All womankind should route 'em,
> But ladies, you must answer too,
> What would we do without 'em?
> Still I hate men![4]

The music accompanying these words is written in steady unrelenting eight notes with a pause after each two lines. The tempo is fast enough to make it difficult to bring out the nuances of meanings of the phrases separated by commas.

One possible solution to a problem such as this is to create the effect of separation that the comma requires by means of a *slight stress on the first syllable of the word following the comma.* Thus:

From all I've read, *a*lone in bed,
From A to Zed, *a*bout 'em,
Since love is blind, *then* from the mind,
All womankind should route 'em,
But ladies, *you* must answer too,
What would we do without 'em?
Still I hate men!

The underlined syllables are to be stressed. Needless to say, the accents are to be subtly pointed, not hammered out lest the effect be mechanical. The performer must also remember that the audience, being at a distance, hears somewhat differently than the singer. It is easy for adjoining words to become slurred. The accenting of syllables as described is one way of avoiding such slurring.

Another example, this one culled from *Candide* (Bernstein and Wilbur), presents a similar problem which will, however, be treated in a different way.

Life is pleasant, life is simple
Oh, my God,/is that a pimple?
No,/it's just the odd reflection
Life and I are still perfection.[5]

The tempo here is faster than in the previous example, and there are no convenient pauses between lines. The effect is one of humorous agitation and frantic concern. The words *God* and *no* are both followed by commas. They are also used in an exclamatory fashion, indicating that they should be stressed. To effect this, we will "cheat" on these words. This means that *God* and *no* will be slightly lengthened, thereby emphasizing both the punctuation and the humor of the lines. To compensate for the loss of tempo that such lengthening entails, the words following the comma-slashes will have to be shortened, telescoped. Again, the degree to which this kind of cheating is done should be governed by an awareness that the flow of the music should be uninterrupted.

The use of a quotation adds drama to written or spoken language because it introduces another character into the scene. We hear a voice other than the speaker's or writer's directly expressed to the listener or reader. Variety and contrast are thus introduced, and interest is heightened. In spite of their significance, quotation marks are often ignored by singers.

A typical example occurs in "Bali Ha'i" (*South Pacific*), in which Bloody Mary, attempting to lure Lieutenant Cable to the island, sings:

> Bali Ha'i may call you any night, any day.
> In your heart you'll hear it call you:
> "Come away, come away."[6]

The quotation marks are most significant, for they indicate that the island itself is speaking. This requires the singer to give the phrase the appropriate coloring and to make clear where the quotation begins and ends. The magical atmosphere of Bali Ha'i needs to be expressed with the eyes, face, gesture, and tone of voice so that there is no doubt when Bloody Mary speaks for herself and when she speaks for the island. Throughout the song, similar quotations occur, giving it a unique quality.

When we listen to the speech of a fine actor, or of anyone who has the talent of expressive utterance, we become aware of the limitless variety of sounds that the human voice can make: No two syllables are pronounced in quite the same way. One hears accents and subaccents, crescendos, and diminuendos, upward and downward inflections, climaxes and low points, resonant or dull sounds, textures and colors of infinite variety. The range of expressivity of the human voice is remarkable, and the development of the color and accent of which it is capable is one of the performer's most important tasks.

Whereas the lyricist can clarify the meaning of his verse through punctuation, thereby giving us a sense of the relative importance of the parts of speech, the only means he has of indicating accentuation is by means of exclamation marks, italicization, underlining, or bold facing particular words. The greatest part of accentuation, stressing, and emphasis—that is, the imparting of the subtleties of meaning—is left for the performer to effect. (The distinction between the three terms is: Accentuation refers to the prominence of a syllable within a word; stress to the prominence of a word within a sentence and emphasis to the prominence of a sentence within a larger group of sentences.)

In the case of punctuation, the intent of the lyricist regarding meaning is usually clear. A comma or semicolon denotes a separation of thought that is unmistakable.

When it comes to accentuation, however, intent becomes more difficult to determine. The literature of both musical theater and popular music is replete with examples of words that will be mis-stressed if pronounced according to their musical placement.

Sometimes such an effect is interesting or humorous. A melody may have such strong rhythmic drive that we do not mind a misplaced accent because the musical logic takes precedence over the lyrical. But at other times, when we are aware of an awkwardness or inappropriateness of misaccentuation, we may assume that the lack of synchrony was not by intent, but rather by lack of skill on the part of the composer or lyricist.

In studying a song, the performer should make careful note of the coming together of musical and lyrical accents. He should note the points at which they do not correspond and evaluate the importance of the musical versus the lyrical accent and determine if an adjustment is necessary. Special attention should also be given to words that fall on the bar line. In many songs there is a natural rhythmic pulse that causes these words to become accentuated. This may or may not be desirable, depending on the characteristic of the song. The following example from "Over The Rainbow" (Arlen and Harburg) illustrates some of the problems that may arise:

*Some*where over the *rain*bow *way* up *high,*
There's a *land* that I heard of once in a *lull*aby.[7]

(The italicized syllables indicate how these lines might be expressively rendered in speech.)

In the song proper, however, a number of misplaced accents occur due to the peaks in the melody and the pulse created by the bar lines. Thus, we hear:

Some*where* over the Rain*bow* way *up* high,
There's *a* land that I heard *of once* in a lullaby.

The long line and beauty of the melody makes us overlook the faulty accentuation. Nevertheless, the singer should be aware of this fact and not compound the problem by accentuating the syllables that are already misaccentuated. Rather, he should soften these musical accents and bring out the lyrical ones. In this way, the discrepancy between the two is minimized and a more natural reading (singing) results.

In "Far From the Home I Love" (*Fiddler on the Roof*), Hodel tries to communicate to her father, Tevye, how painful her decision is to leave her home and family. She struggles to make him "under*stand*." When set to music, however, the word "understand" falls on the downbeat of a measure, thereby becoming "*un*derstand," a misaccentuation. The correction consists of reaccenting the word by restoring the stress on the last syllable while meticulously observing the written note values.

A similar situation occurs in the line "Why I do what I do."

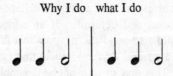

Why I do   what I do

Here again, the strong downbeats cause *why* and *what* to become overstressed. By restressing the phrase according to natural speech, the line becomes more flowing and dramatically more congruent.

In the example that follows, the lyricist not only mis-stresses the words, but does so intentionally for the sake of playful whimsy or to produce unusual rhymes:

> Although he may not be the *man some*
> Girls think of as *handsome* . . . [8]

In "The Man I Love" (George and Ira Gershwin) *Tuesday* is made to rhyme with *news day,* and in "Bill" (P.G. Wodehouse, Oscar Hammerstein II, and Jerome Kern), we find *statue* coupled with *that you* and *roomy* with *to me.*

[8]"Someone to Watch Over Me" by George and Ira Gershwin. © 1926 New World Music Corporation. Copyright Renewed. All Rights Reserved. Used by Permission of Warner Bros. Music.

Such deliberately forced rhymes were very much in vogue during the 1920s and 1930s, and now we tend to look upon them as period pieces. Nonetheless, the intent of the lyricist should, I think, be respected, and the words stressed accordingly.

Then there is the intentionally misplaced accentuation that results when words are willingly subordinated to strongly rhythmic music. In such cases, the drive of the rhythmic motif takes precedence over everything else, the words often taking a repetitive pattern that reinforces the music.

> *I* got rhythm
> *I* got music
> *I* got my man
> Who could ask for anything more?[9]

It can be seen from the above examples that although the composer and lyricist generally try to coordinate musical and lyrical accents so thay they support the grammatical structure of the text, exceptions abound. The performer's task is to correctly interpret the intention of the lyric. If he judges that the accentuation and rhyme schemes are intended to be stylistic, entertaining, or unusual, he should perform the song accordingly. On the other hand, if he determines the lyric to be more naturalistic (more like everyday speech), he should compensate for any misaccentuation, as in the example of "Far From The Home I Love."

Exercise

Take a ballad that is familiar to you and sing it through. (If possible, use a cassette recorder to track your progress.) Give it your best shot, for you will use it later for comparison.

Now, using the lyrics alone, speak them out loud. Do not phrase them metrically; ignore the meter of the lines. Be free, lengthening or shortening words, making pauses when they seem to be needed. Let the pacing come from your individual response to the meaning and feeling of the words.

Speak the lyrics a second time. Notice which words you are stressing; note the rise and fall of inflections, pacing and energy. Where does your energy seem to peak? Where do you breathe?

Now transfer all these observations to your sheet music. Indicate the words that are stressed, inflected, and so on. Use whatever notation works for you.

Once you have found the reading that satisfies you, the music and lyrics can be joined together. Now perform the song in its entirety, being careful to retain the nuances that emerged from the reading. The addition of the melody will now enhance and reinforce the text, resulting in a more meaningful performance. Compare this with your initial effort.

It is worth repeating the caution that once the song is put together, there is a strong tendency to revert to habitual ways of performing. The act of singing usually triggers a series of automatic responses—facial expressiong associated with "placing" the tone, stereotyped enunciation, upright singing posture, and so forth. All these will tend to neutralize what the exercise attempts to achieve: an individual expression of the text.

Retelling
the Lyric

3

If you had difficulty making the last exercise in Chapter 2 sound natural and unaffected, the cause may have been any of the following:

- The rhythm and rhymes of the lyric exerted a pull, and you found yourself falling back into reading poetry.
- The lines sounded memorized rather than uttered for the first time. (This is a difficulty that all actors struggle with—how to keep lines fresh and spontaneous sounding.)
- You were reading about someone else's experience rather than your own. It was not personal.

An effective way of overcoming these difficulties is to improvise your own version of the lyric. Everyone is to some extent a storyteller. We all do it every day of our lives. Naturally, some are better than others, but that doesn't matter. The point is to personalize a lyric.

Exercise

Speaking in the first person, create a little soliloquy in which you retell the story of the lyric in your own words. Let it come out in any way that is easy or natural for you. Don't try to be poetic. Use the ordinary everyday language you find comfortable. Sincerity and spontaneity are the goals. Try to relate your improvisation to a personal experience and allow your feelings to become involved.

If you have a pianist at your disposal, let her or him play the song so that it serves as background for your improvisation. Be sensitive to the mood of the music and allow it to play on your feelings. As you do this, you may find dormant memories of past events entering your consciousness, and your personal feelings may become involved.

Example

(1)If I loved you,
Time and again I would try to say
All I'd want you to know.
If I loved you,
(5)Words wouldn't come in an easy way.
Round in circles I'd go!
Longin' to tell you, but afraid and shy,
I'd let my golden chances pass me by.
Soon you'd leave me,
(10)Off you would go in the mist of day,
Never, never to know
How I loved you,
If I loved you.[1]

Retelling the Lyric: "If I loved you, I guess I'd have a really hard time telling you how I felt; I wouldn't know how. Oh, maybe I'd ask you to have a cup of coffee with me or go to a ball game. But you'd never know what was going on inside of me. Then, one day maybe you'd meet some other guy who you liked a lot, and he'd ask you to go with him to another town and get married. And off you'd go—me saying goodbye to you like it didn't matter much. And you'd never know that I was in love with you— that is, if I *was* in love with you, which, of course, I'm not."

It is important in all the suggested exercises that you perform them completely. Do not be content to merely read the lyrics, but act them out. Let your body become involved and feel free to move as it seems appropriate. If this seems difficult for you, begin by making random movements. Walk around as you say the lines; look out of the window; pick an object off the floor, or arrange your hair. This will help loosen you up and get away from stereotypical readings. In time, the random movements will give way to meaningful ones. The aim is to open yourself up to new possibilities and more choices—to break down the self-imposed barriers that cause you to express yourself in repetitive ways.

THE CORE MEANING OF THE LYRIC

It must be clear by now that in order to extract the maximum value from a lyric, great care must be taken to determine its content. The singing actor's study of lyrics is not unlike the straight actor studying the script in the preparation of a role, giving the same detailed attention to interpretation as the actor does. The comparative brevity of most lyrics merely underscores their highly concentrated nature and the correspondingly greater importance of each word.

The performer can carry the process of concentrating on lyrical meaning further. By paring off all unessential verbal elements, the lyric can be reduced to one or two sentences that contain the gist of what it is about. Everyone will do this in his or her own way and arrive at a different result. This is good because a personal interpretation is desired.

The benefits of this exercise for the performer are several: First, it is a powerful mental discipline to learn to discriminate between the essential and nonessential elements of language, whether written or spoken. After all, communication and understanding between people is based on this ability. Secondly, by compressing the lyric to its most elementary expression, the performer forges a tool with which to keep his concentration alive. Finally, it encourages him to think of what it is he is singing about.

Exercise

Take the same lyric you worked on in the retelling exercise and apply the above described procedure. Eliminate any lines that seem expendable and continue reducing the lyric until you are left with one or two statements that seem irreducible. (Often the title of the song will be such a statement.)

Out of these remaining sentences or fragments of sentences, formulate your own summation. Try different ways until you arrive at one that fits and seems true to you. This will be your core meaning. Some examples follow:

- "Far From the Home I Love" *(Fiddler On The Roof);* Core Meaning (CM): "It hurts to leave you, knowing that you don't understand."
- "If I Loved You" *(Carousel);* (CM): "I love you, but I'm scared that you might not love me back."
- "Feelin' Good" *(The Roar of The Greasepaint);* (CM): "It's great to be alive."
- "The Party's Over" *(Bells Are Ringing);* (CM): "I've got to wake up to reality and go on."

It goes without saying that these core sentences are personal choices, varying a great deal from individual to individual.

The core meaning is to be used during performance to act as a persistent theme that pervades the performer's consciousness. We are often haunted by such persistent thoughts in real life, especially in stressful situations. For example, in looking for a lost child our minds might be filled with the thought, "it's my fault—it's my fault."

As you sing, allow this motif sentence to hover behind the lyrics, becoming more prominent in the spaces between musical phrases or during interludes when you are silent. Let yourself be aware of it especially *before* you begin to sing, while the introduction is being played.

Imagery

4

The ability to transform descriptive words and figures of speech into mental images is inherent in us. A vivid phrase or metaphor can not only cause us to "see" and "hear" with our mind's eye and ear, it can create bodily sensations as well. Thus a passage describing warmth and happiness makes our muscles relax, and if we are sensitive to our bodies, we may actually feel a sensation of warmth. A description of conflict or pain will contract our muscles and perhaps make us clench our hands.

The performer who allows himself to respond to imagery will find his mind as well as his body reacting to the images. It is through these visible, external signs that the audience knows what a performer is experiencing: The random movements of his eyes reflect his inner experience; his facial muscles relax and contract in accordance with feelings that are aroused by the images. The performer's body language conveys to the audience his various mental states as expressed through attitudes, tensions, and relaxations. Finally, the audience hears through the performer's voice and its varying shades of timbre and pitch fluctuations the aural reflection of the images.

(It must be remembered, however, that these responses depend on the image taking hold in the mind to begin with. If the image is not truly experienced and the body reactions merely mimicked, the result is mechanical and the audience discovers the deception immediately.)

A few illustrations follow:

> There's a bright, golden haze on the meadow,
> There's a bright, golden haze on the meadow,
> The corn is as high as an elephant's eye,
> An' it looks like it's climbin' clear up to the sky.[1]

The first line evokes a vivid mental picture of a lovely natural setting. The reference to bright colors and open expanses should induce a feeling of warmth, contentment, and well-being which, in turn, will probably bring on a smile and a sense of relaxation in the body. In the third line, the image of "The corn is as high as an elephant's eye" is so fanciful that humor is mixed with astonishment. And the fourth line, "An' it looks like it's climbin' clear up to the sky," stretches the imagination even further by introducing an image which might bring to mind an association with "Jack And The Beanstalk." The piling up of images, each one more extreme than the one before, will register in the performer's eyes and face, and the audience will then see what he sees.

When Louisa, in *Fantasticks*, sings the following lines, the imagery is both visual and tactile:

> I'd like to swim in a clear blue stream
> Where the water is icy cold:
> Then go to town in a golden gown,
> And have my fortune told.[2]

The mental picture of icy cold water may cause a contraction in the body which could, in turn, stimulate a hunching of the singer's shoulders or a clasping of her arms around herself.

In "The Party's Over" *(Bells Are Ringing)*, figurative language is used with telling effect.

> The party's over.
> It's time to call it a day.
> They've burst your pretty balloon.
> And taken the moon away.[3]

By means of metaphor—speaking of something as if it were something else—the end of a relationship is compared to the end of a party; the implication being that the affair, like a party, was not meant to last. The last two lines evoke the image of a child deprived of her toys, alone and unhappy. It would be natural for the image to trigger a sensation of inner shrinking.

Examine the following songs for their imagery:

"The Sound of Music" *(The Sound of Music)*
"Younger Than Springtime" *(South Pacific)*
"It Might As Well Be Spring" *(State Fair)*

The two great obstacles to active imaging are memorization and repetition. Both are unavoidable in learning any skill, yet the performer must create the illusion of experiencing something for the first time. How can this be done? A great deal depends on the work habits the performer develops when he practices. Mechanical practice will result in mechanical performances. Words must always be translated into experiences, lest they remain dead symbols. Every repetition of a phrase should be a search for a new discovery, nuance, insight, or fresh association. A continual recreation of the song must take place. It is also important to take careful note of first impressions and store away that original, fresh response that a song evoked on first hearing and try to recapture that arousal.

---

[3]"The Party's Over," by Betty Comden, Adolph Green, and Jule Styne. Copyright © 1956 by Betty Comden, Adolph Green & Jule Styne. Stradford Music Corp., owner and Chappell & Co., Inc., Administrator of publication and allied rights for the Western Hemisphere. International Copyright Secured. ALL RIGHTS RESERVED. Used by permission.

Imagination

5

There is no such thing as actuality on the stage. Art is a product of the imagination, as the work of a dramatist should be. The aim of the actor should be to use his technique to turn the play into a theatrical reality. In this process imagination plays by far the greatest part.[1]

It is obvious that these remarks also apply to the singing actor.

The aim of performing is not to present reality—reality is the singer, standing on stage, singing to an audience—but to share with an audience an imagined situation embodying common truths. The song presents the situation; the singer fills it out with imagination.

The raw materials of the imagination are the sum total life experiences of the individual as well as the thoughts, writings, and actions of

[1]Constantin Stanislavski, *An Actor Prepares*, p. 51. Copyright © 1936 by Theatre Arts, Inc. Copyright © by Elizabeth R. Hapgood. All rights reserved under Pan-American Copyright Union. Copyright under International Copyright Union. Used by permission of the publisher, Theatre Arts Books, 153 Waverly Place, New York, N.Y. 10014.

other individuals, past or present. All are a part of the storehouse of experiences from which the imagination can draw.

That we are all endowed with this ability seems unquestionable: Watching children at play, we are reminded how easily and naturally we can invent a world of make-believe and shape it to our liking. Nevertheless, this inborn gift is diminished in many individuals.

The reason for this diminution is to be found in our way of life. The extreme materialism that surrounds us, the gadgetry that solves every problem, television, and the paucity of artistic stimulation all contribute in diminishing our creative powers and making us duller, more passive, and less alive. In our culture there is also a strong judgmental attitude toward anything that is not immediately productive. This certainly pertains to any kind of daydreaming or mind wandering, creative though it may be.

Even though it may be atrophied through neglect, the imagination *can* be reactivated by a conscious, systematic effort of the mind, which like any part of the body, thrives on continuous functioning. The importance of this cannot be exaggerated. Without the active participation of the imagination and the improvisational freedom that goes with it, the performance of a song remains a lifeless sequence of words and notes that cannot possibly communicate anything meaningful to an audience.

The imagination can be prodded in numerous ways. Some of the following suggestions are based on literary or linguistic devices, some on the exploration of sensory experiences, and others on games of various kinds.

1. *Imagery* in language. This has been discussed in the previous pages.
2. *Exaggeration.* The ability of the imagination to enlarge or distort reality is common knowledge. Exaggeration is an essential component of comedy, caricature, folk tales and myths. The so-called tall stories are examples of comic exaggeration.
3. *Fantasizing.* A way of toying with the future. When we fantasize, we create a world of what might be.
4. *Memories.* The replaying of past experiences is another form of imaginative activity that enriches the performer's expressiveness. (Memories of sensations are of special importance.)
5. *Dreams.* Since our inhibitions are relaxed during the dreaming state, dreams represent the ultimate extension of the imagination. Hence, the recalling and the dwelling on the subject matter of dreams is a valuable exercise.
6. *Puns.* Although considered by some to be a low form of humor, puns nevertheless are mind expanders, since they are based on double meanings and ambiguity. (Shakespeare, doubtlessly, was the greatest punster of all.)

7. *Charades* and other such games that depend on the acting out of names, phrases, or situations also encourage inventiveness.

8. *Anagrams* and *crossword puzzles.*

9. *Improvised storytelling* is another creative activity. A story can be begun as simply as "Once upon a time." An interesting variant of this game is for two people to share in the extemporization—one person starting, the other continuing, the first again picking up the story, and so on.

Following are some exercises that have been found useful in encouraging creative mind wandering.

Reactivating the Imagination

Take an ordinary object such as a pencil or a cup. If you're outdoors you might choose a rock, a flower, or a tree.

Examine the object in great detail for several minutes. Observe its component parts: its color, weight, texture, taste, how it reflects light, and so on.

Now let your imagination play with the object. Allow associations and comparisons to come into your mind; let thoughts and impressions freely float into your consciousness and take their own course. Perhaps the dimensions of the object will change and become huge or tiny; perhaps the pencil will become a spear or an animal. The tree might become a person, or the cup might become the mouth of an active volcano. Enjoy discovering the transformations as they surface in your mind.

Now endow the object with human emotions: the angry tree, the loving flower, the jealous cup, or the obstinate rock.

Now invent a reason why the tree is angry or the flower is loving. Perhaps the tree is angry because a lightning bolt has knocked off one of its branches, or another tree has been spreading malicious gossip about it. The flower may be loving because a bee has just brought it a message of love from another flower.

Let this exercise be done without the need to accomplish anything; let it merely be a free-floating fantasy. Allow it to go as far as it wants to go and stop when it runs dry.

More Imaginings

If you could be an animal, which one would you choose? A dog, a weasel, a gazelle? Choose one. Now imagine yourself as this animal. Go into great detail in describing your existence. Speak of yourself in the first person and in the present tense. Talk about the food you eat, where you sleep, how you try to escape from your enemies. What are your characteristics? Are you cautious, bold, fearful, or clownish? Conceive of your friends as other animals, each with his or her characteristics. Perhaps you can get a friend to role-play the other animal. Don't stick to stereotypes like bold lion or gentle lamb. Perhaps a toothless snake or gossiping grasshopper comes to mind. Be open to any idea.

Still imagining yourself as this particular animal, do an improvisation, either playing all the parts by yourself or with the help of a friend. Suggested improvisations include a children's playground, a court trial with defending and prosecuting lawyers arguing a case, or a family squabble involving a problem teenager.

Variations on this improvisation: if you were a vehicle, what would you be? A Cadillac limousine, a skateboard, a motorcycle, a horse-drawn buggy? If you were a food, what kind would you be? A steak, a health salad, a cream puff? Elaborate the details as above.

THE USE
OF SUPPOSITION

When we look at our own lives in retrospect, going back as far as we can remember, they seem to be filled with an endless succession of experiences. We have passed through stages of learning in order to use our bodies and minds. We have had relationships with a number of people, who have affected us in various ways. We have mastered certain skills. At present, we are at a particular state of our lives, in transition to another stage. All in all, much seems to have happened.

Yet when we look around and compare ourselves with the rest of humanity and become aware of the limitless range of human experience, our own lives may seem dull and uneventful. We begin to think of all the things we have *not* done, the abilities we do *not* have, the exciting adventures that have *not* happened to us, the great love of our lives who has *not* come. We suffer from a sense of loss and deprivation.

But suppose you were a figure of great authority; how would you act? Suppose you were a guttersnipe; how would you take care of yourself? Suppose the great love of your life were to walk into the room; how would you feel?

Suddenly our world expands, our vision widens, and the impossible becomes, in our imagination, possible.

Supposition has the following functions:

1. By setting the actor's imagination in motion, it enables him to enlarge his experience and step into someone else's existence, imagining what he would do *if* he were the other person.
2. It enables him to imagine the outcome of any act, his own or another's, by saying, "If this were to happen, I would. . . ."
3. It clarifies the problem of what is "real" on stage. The actor is an actor, playing a part. He and his feelings are as real as the stage, costumes, and scenery. The rest of it—the play, the characters and the stage action—are all a *supposed reality.* There is no conflict between the two. They coexist.

Exercise

Take a newspaper or magazine and randomly pick out a story that describes a person who is in some way quite different from you.

> A very tall or short person
> Someone having a serious illness
> A great athlete or a physical weakling
> Someone very rich or poor
> A criminal or a preacher
> A statesman or a politician
> A housewife or a working man

Put yourself in the place of that person and imagine what *you* would do if the particular circumstances of the article had happened to you.

Every role you play and every song you sing is an exercise in the use of supposition. We do not need to be taught how to suppose an imagined circumstance; It comes to us quite naturally. However, we can learn to increase the range of our imaginings by consciously venturing into areas that are more and more removed from our actual lives.

FANTASY JOURNEYS

Fantasy journeys can lead you to new experiences and insights.

The Empty House: Sit in a comfortable chair in a quiet part of the house. Close your eyes and breathe calmly. Become aware of any tension in your body and try to relax it away. Do this for a minute or two.

Now imagine that you are in a room in a strange house. Everything is unfamiliar to you. There is a door in front of you. You have a great curiosity and/or apprehension to know what is behind that door. You open the door slowly and walk through. What do you encounter? Allow yourself to flow with your fantasy. Perhaps there are other rooms with strange furnishings. You may meet someone. Do you want to ask that person questions? Perhaps there is only emptiness. Whatever there is, let it be.

You may want to record your journey onto a cassette recorder.

Meeting the Child: As before, make yourself comfortable and relax. Imagine that you are on a lonely beach. It's a warm, sunny day and you walk along the shore, enjoying the sound of the waves splashing on the sand. As you continue to walk, you notice a small figure in the distance. Coming closer, you see that it is a child, playing in the sand. You realize that the child is you. Start a conversation, asking the child how things are, how it feels about its parents, and so forth. The child, in turn, asks about you. When you have finished talking, say goodbye to the child and leave. As you walk away, turn your head to look behind you at the child. What is he or she doing?

The Undersea Exploration: You are skin diving in a tropical sea near the shore of some strange land. There are fantastic creatures and plants all around you. In the dim light that filters through the water, you see a huge shape, half buried in the sand of the ocean floor. It looks very ancient, like a sunken ship. You explore the deck and the interior. What was its cargo? What objects do you find? What are your feelings as you go through the ship?

Before you leave the ship to return to shore, you are allowed to take one thing with you. Decide what you want. Notice how you feel about your choice.

IMPROVISED ROLE-PLAYING

One of the most interesting and surprising experiences in life is discovering that we know more than we thought we knew, that we had hidden knowledge. We read a book and come across a passage that seems to us singularly meaningful and true, and something inside of us says, "Yes, I *know.*" The author perhaps states the idea with a clarity and sublety that we could not duplicate; nevertheless, we experience an intuitive recognition of something we have known all along. What is curious about this is that so many of our insights remain unacknowledged until they are brought to light by some such stimulus. Why is this so? I believe it has to do with the nature of the thinking process and the changes that this process undergoes when it is expressed in speech or writing.

Except when it is engaged in problem-solving, thinking is most often a discontinuous, random process, lacking in logical sequence. Our thoughts jump from subject to subject as various stimuli influence us, resulting in a mixture of fragmentary fantasies and memories.

However, when thought is expressed through speech or writing, several important elements are introduced. For one thing, our thoughts are now externalized, and we can hear or see them. This alone is vital, since we now have a feedback mechanism that gives us the opportunity of correcting ourselves. Merely speaking our thoughts aloud—which is a soliloquy—is to better understand ourselves.

Speech in the form of dialogue takes us one step further, for now we not only hear ourselves and respond to our own feedback, but we respond to that of our partner. This process includes justification of our point of view, rational argument, and correctly interpreting our partner's verbal and nonverbal messages such as body language and tone of voice. It is in dialogue, especially when speaking with an intimate, that our hidden inner wisdom often emerges. Words of practical common sense and on-target sagacity spring from us spontaneously. We are sensitive to the emotional state of our friend; we are aware of contradictory statements being made and are quick to point out flaws in reasoning. We are also able to listen—all this assuming that an open, nondefensive feeling between the participants exists—to similar comments regarding ourselves and are able to see ourselves more clearly.

Intimate dialoguing, or role-playing, is a unique learning tool for the performer. Its purpose is to broaden the concept of a character or a song by playing out the opposing ends of any particular situation. The interaction of the two participants acts as a catalyst which activates rational as well as emotional elements that are inherent in the situation. Because the role-playing is the acting out of an imaginary situation, the atmosphere is non-threatening, the defenses of the participants are lowered, and conditions are thus ripe for our inner wisdom to emerge.

Improvised role-playing can be practiced in two ways. In the first, the performer acts out both roles, alternately playing one role, then the other, as if there were two separate individuals. In the second, the roles are played by two individuals, necessitating the help of a fellow performer.

When to use this device? Whenever an inadequacy is felt regarding the depth or range of a character; when a song feels not quite fulfilled; when there is some doubt about the meaning of the lyric; or when the performer finds it difficult to relate to the song with sufficient empathy.

The dialogue can be held between (1) performer and character, (2) character and character, and (3) character and object.

Dialogue Between Performer and Character

The Performer: John, a singing actor playing the part of Littlechap in *Stop The World, I Want To Get Off*

The Character: Littlechap, a little man intent on overcoming his mean origin, who has scratched and clawed his way to the top of the social ladder. He also realizes at this moment that in the course of the struggle he has lost something precious.

John: Littlechap, I find it hard to understand you and relate to you. You're so coarse and insensitive. You have no respect for anyone else's needs. I despise you.

L.C.: Who the hell are you to come on to me like that? So you think you're more sensitive, more honest, do you? Well, I know you better, and you don't fool me a bit. You've got a streak of cruelty just like me; you just like to hide it.

John: That's a lie. Why, some of the things you've done just to get ahead, the deceit, the cruelty you've been guilty of make me sick.

L.C.: Listen to Mr. High and Mighty. How about the time you played up to that girl at that party down in the Village? Remember what happened? And what about those so-called business expenses that you claim on your income tax? You're not so lily-white after all, it seems.

John: Yeah, I'd rather not remember some of those things. Maybe we're not so unalike after all.

L.C.:   Also, I don't appreciate your remarks right now, when I'm feeling pretty bad about myself and the things I've done.

John: I'm sorry. I'm not feeling good about myself either.

This example of an improvised dialogue could obviously go on at great length, both sides exploring the similarities and differences of their characters and values. If the dialogue has been honest and self-disclosing, it should bring the two parties into a closer relationship and give John a more empathetic understanding of Littlechap. This, in turn, will strongly affect the interpretation of "What Kind of Fool Am I?" which Littlechap sings at the end of the show.

Dialogue Between
Character and Character

In "As Long As He Needs Me" from *Oliver,* Nancy (character 1) describes her tortured relationship with Bill Sykes (character 2) and tries to justify why she sticks it out with him. She says a great deal about her feelings for him and of her need to be needed. But we know very little about Bill and his feelings.

Create a dialogue between them based on the above model. Let them speak their thoughts and feelings. Let them accuse, defend, justify, and answer each other. Let them state their needs and frustrations as openly as possible. When the dialogue ends, Nancy sings "As Long As He Needs Me."

The dialoguing between characters is based on the same idea as retelling the lyric: Having to use your own words, your sense of yourself as the character and your relationship to other characters becomes clearer and more meaningful.

Dialogue Between
Character and Object

In *The Most Happy Fella,* Joey is an itinerant farm worker, a drifter who feels he's been too long in one place, and that it's time to move on. In the song "Joey, Joey, Joey" he imagines the wind "like a perfumed woman," enticing him to find greener pastures. The improvised role-playing might go like this:

> Joey: I'm getting tired of this place, tired of the same people, the same chores. Now that the harvest is done, there's nothing to keep me here. I sure can't see myself settlin' down in a place like this.
>
> The Wind: Joey, come along with me. I wander all over the earth; over mountains, valleys, seas, and deserts. I don't have to answer to anybody. I'm completely free. But sometimes I get lonesome and need some company. Hey, Joey, I could show you some fantastic sights if you would let me. Come with me, that's it, come. Now we're crossing the desert. Look down there to your left; do you see that?
>
> Joey: Yeh. Say, that looks like it could be Arizona. Is it? I sure remember some good times I had there. Maybe I could help bring in the sugar beet crop.

The performer will find interesting differences in playing both roles and having another person playing one of them opposite him. The other person will naturally bring his own experience and background into the dialogue and respond in an entirely different manner.

Emotion

6

Everyone experiences emotional states in everyday life, varying from mild annoyance to murderous rage, from slight disappointment to devastating grief. Though the average person has little self-knowledge about what occurs when he is emotional, the actor (singer) must know a great deal about it, since emotion is one of the principal ingredients of drama (song).

Without going into psychological jargon, several things can be stated on the subject.

1. Emotion can be defined as a state of arousal (pleasant or unpleasant) when certain bodily changes occur: The blood pressure fluctuates, skin tone changes, visceral sensations are felt, and muscles contract or relax. These physical changes are accompanied by mental states that are variously labeled fear, anger, love, and hate.

2. Emotion is an involuntary response to a stimulus or event. Someone insults you and you become angry. Someone gives you a gift and you feel gratitude.

3. Once aroused, emotion moves us to act: You retaliate against the person who has insulted you or show appreciation to the giver of the gift. Yet, though there is an impulse to act, it may be inhibited. Consequently, instead of retaliating against the insult, you may merely fantasize the retaliation because of fear. Embarrassment may prevent you from showing gratitude.

4. The inhibition of emotion is taught to every individual early in life. We are urged to keep our feelings hidden, especially negative ones. "Don't cry," "don't be angry," "don't show sexual feelings" and other "don'ts" create a dichotomy of emotion on one hand and concealment on the other.

5. Extreme emotion can result in the loss of self-control. Our language illustrates this with expressions such as "blew his top," "crazy in love," "freaked out," and "blind rage."

The actor's position regarding emotion is a paradoxical one: as a human being, he is subject to the conditions previously outlined, but as an actor the awareness of what his character feels must be constant. When his character inhibits or conceals an emotion, the actor knows why. When his character loses control in an explosion of anger, the actor stays in control and guides him through the scene. The actor allows his feelings to become involved; they are "real," but so is the stage, the costumes, and the scenery. There is a shuttling back and forth between two kinds of reality. At times the intellect leads the action; at other times feelings predominate. A state of being may also be reached in a performance where awareness is completely extinguished. During such moments, the performer stops "acting" and sheds his own identity; he does what needs to be done in the most effortless manner, without seeming to make decisions or choices. Interestingly, the performer is often not conscious of doing anything special during such moments—"it" simply happens.

The first exercise on emotion, which involves naming the feeling in a lyric may seem rather simplistic at first glance, but its value will become apparent. It consists of giving a name to the feelings that underlie a lyric.

Lyrics, of course, differ greatly from one another not only in the variety of emotional content, but in the relative simplicity or complexity of the emotions. For example, "I Got Rhythm," (George and Ira Gershwin) expresses a simple feeling of joyous exuberance throughout the song. Similarly, "Stormy Weather," (Arlen and Koehler) is uncomplicated in its feelings of sadness and loss. On the other hand, such pieces as "Sorry-Grateful" and "Barcelona" by Stephen Sondheim are full of mixed and conflicting feelings. (Sondheim has a particular fondness for ambivalence, and his scores are replete with examples of this theme.)

By giving a name to the feelings expressed in a lyric, the performer commits himself to an attitude. Starting with very general descriptions and then becoming more and more specific in the terms that are used, the performer develops an awareness of the emotional nuances behind the words.

Exercise

Examine a lyric and determine what characterizes its mood or emotional tone. Describe this in a word or two, in the manner of a stage direction to a play, e.g., "angrily—with determination—gratefully," and so on. Write these words over the lyrics on the sheet music. Do this each time you notice the slightest change in mood or feeling. When singing the song, observe the descriptive notations you have made, and interpret the lyric accordingly.

Be aware that there is no one interpretation for any song, so don't hesitate to change your interpretation if a better idea suggests itself. However, do not dilute an interpretation by trying to combine two opposing concepts. Strength lies in singleness of viewpoint.

"Much More"

This piece from the *Fantasticks* is unusual in the number of contrasting mood changes it exhibits.

(excitedly)
I'd like to swim in a clear blue stream where the water is icy cold.

(daringly)
Then go to town in a golden gown and have my fortune told.

(pleadingly)
Just once. Just once.

(with pathos)
Just once before I'm old.

(explaining)
I'd like to be not evil but a little worldly wise.

(romantically)
To be the kind of girl designed to be kissed upon the eyes.

(wildly)
I'd like to dance til two o'clock or sometimes dance til dawn.

(more and more carried away)
Or if the band could stand it, just go on and on and on.

(pleadingly)
Just once, just once.

(self-pityingly)
Before the chance is gone.[1]

"Who Can I Turn To"[2]

The opening line, "Who can I turn to when nobody needs me?" suggests *despair* and *hopelessness* (note this on your music). The lyric continues in this vein until the 17th bar, where it states: "And maybe tomorrow I'll know what I'm after." Here a ray of *hopefulness* seems to illuminate the darkness. This hopefulness continues until the last four bars: "But who can I turn to if you turn away?" A *desperate plea* ends the song. (The italicized words are to be written over the appropriate lyrics.)

"Far From the Home I Love"

(pleadingly)
How can I hope to make you understand
Why I do what I do,

(with pain and regret)
Why I must travel to a distant land
Far from the home I love?[3]

"If I Loved You"

(shyly)
If I loved you,
Time and again I would try to say
All I'd want you to know.

(hopeful that he'll understand)
If I loved you,
Words wouldn't come in an easy way—

(self-deprecating)
Round in circles I'd go![4]

(Remember that these descriptive terms are personal to the author; yours
may differ.)

Following is a list of words that illustrates the range and diversity of
feelings. Add your own words to the list.

abandoned	blaming	confused
abashed	blissful	content
adamant	bold	contrite
affectionate	bored	cruel
aglow	brave	crushed
agonized	bullying	
alarmed		deceitful
ambivalent	calm	defeated
angry	callous	defensive
annoyed	capable	delighted
anxious	captivated	desolate
apathetic	carnal	despairing
astounded	charmed	despising
awed	chaste	destructive
	cheated	determined
baffled	cheerful	diffident
beautiful	childish	diminished
betrayed	clever	depressed
biting	combative	discontented
bitter	condemned	distracted

distraught
disturbed
divided
dominated
doubtful

eager
ecstatic
eerie
electrified
enchanted
enervated
envious
erotic
excited
evil
exasperated
exhausted

fascinated
fawning
fearful
flustered
foolish
foreboding
forgiving
frantic
frightened
frustrated
furious
furtive

gay
glad
gleeful
grateful
greedy
grievous
groovy
guilty

happy
hateful
haughty
heavenly

helpless
helpful
high
homesick
horrible
hot-blooded
hurt
hysterical

ignored
impressed
indignant
indulgent
infatuated
infuriated
inspired
intimidated
isolated

jaded
jealous
joyous
jumpy

keen
kind
kinky

lazy
lecherous
lively
loathing
lonely
longing
loving
lustful

mad
maternal
maudlin
mean
melancholy
menacing
miserable
mystical

naughty
nervous
nice
niggardly
nutty

obnoxious
obsessed
obstinate
odd
ominous
outraged
overwhelmed

pained
panicked
peaceful
persecuted
petrified
pitiful
pious
playful
pleased
precarious
pressured
prim
proud
puny

quarrelsome
queer

rabid
raging
raptured
reckless
refreshed
rejected
relaxed
relieved
remorseful
restless
reproachful
righteous
rousing

sad	stunned	uneasy
sarcastic	stupefied	unsettled
sated	suffering	
satisfied	sure	vehement
scared	sympathetic	vengeful
screwed up		violent
servile	tempted	vital
settled	tenacious	vivacious
sexy	tense	vulnerable
shocked	terrified	
shot down	threatened	wacky
sickened	thrilled	warm
silly	thwarted	weepy
skeptical	tortured	whimsical
slavish	trapped	wicked
sneaky	trifled	wild
solemn	troubled	wonderful
sorrowful		worried
spiteful	ugly	
startled	unconquerable	zany
stingy	understanding	zapped

What was your experience with the preceding exercise? Did you actually feel the emotions that you had written over the lyrics, or did you give an imitation of an emotion and put on a mask of excitement, sorrow, or joy?

To evoke a true feeling rather than mimicking one is a common difficulty for both beginner and professional; it is so much easier to paste on a smile of happiness or to turn the corners of the mouth down in simulated sadness than to involve oneself. Unfortunately, the simulation fools no one. The most uneducated member of the audience can see through the attempted deception. At best, they will admire your skill, but they can hardly become involved unless you are.

There are valid reasons why we would rather not show our real feelings to the world. Society urges us to censor, edit, or eliminate entirely the expression of our most basic feelings. If you are hurt and cry, you are called weak. If someone humiliates you and you become angry, you are being unreasonable. If someone turns you on sexually, you may be labeled "dirty."

Although there are considerable social pressures that encourage the individual to censor, edit, or entirely suppress some feelings, the singer/actor, paradoxically, is praised and applauded for being open and showing feelings. Yet even this reward is usually insufficient to overcome the great resistance to self-disclosure that most of us have. There is seeming safety in hiding behind a mask and a corresponding sense of danger in removing it.

Since the inhibition of emotion is so strongly conditioned and cannot be commanded—it is not possible to say "I will now fall in love" or "I will now become angry" and actually *feel* love or anger—the actor must discover indirect ways to arouse the appropriate feelings.

There are three basic ways of doing this: identification, emotional recall, and physicalization.

The first two are based on a primarily mental process. By means of comparisons, associations, and memories that have an emotional charge, the performer establishes a connecting link with the contents of the lyrics. A transference of emotion is thus produced. This, in turn, becomes visible in such signs as changes of skin tone and coloring, muscular contraction, relaxation, and physical movement. The actor is then aware of feelings such as love or anger.

Physicalization uses a contrary approach: Instead of starting from the inside (mind), it begins with some physical act that is directly associated with the emotion. As in the first two methods, a chain reaction is initiated. This time, the physical act triggers an emotional response, which, in turn, produces the previously mentioned outward signs.

EVOKING EMOTION

To observe the differences among people is to learn the uniqueness of individuals, that each is an original creation, never to be exactly duplicated.

By contrast, the study of similarities reveals the common traits that link all human beings and that make communication and understanding between them possible.

The awareness of similarities—especially those of character traits and social values—tends to bond individuals or groups with others that have like traits and values, and "identification" takes place. To identify with someone (confining ourselves to interpersonal relationships for the present), is to feel the same as, to put yourself in the place of, to empathize with that person.

For the singer/actor, identification is the means of establishing lines of communication between himself and his character. As these lines multiply, the bonding becomes firmer until actor and character overlap and blend. (Though identification in itself is not an emotion, it can become a bridge to emotion if the connection touches on a sensitive area.)

Exercise

Take an inanimate object and name some trait in it with which you can identify. Make your own identification with these and other objects.

- I am like a stone in that I can be hard and unyielding at times.
- I am like water in that I flow in whatever direction the land goes.
- I am like a house in that I provide comfort for people.
- I am like an empty house in that I feel useless.
- I am like a wall in that I'm stubborn and make people climb over me.
- I am like an oak tree in that I am solid and dependable.

Find similar identifying connections with an animal. Finding two or more identifications expands the imagination.

- I am like a cat in that I'm independent.
- I am like a sparrow in that I'm ordinary.
- I am like a frog in that people think I'm funny.
- I am like a frog in that I'm very adaptable.

As before, make your own connections and add to the list.

Exercise

Choose a character from a musical. First make a list of the character's general traits and note the ones that are common to you. For instance, you might characterize Hodel in *Fiddler On The Roof* as strong-willed, honest, loving, or committed. Can you identify with any of these qualities?

Next, take a specific situation in the play, for instance, when Hodel tries to make her father understand why she is leaving home and sings "Far From the Home I Love." Search for a connection between that situation and something similar in your own life.

In what ways can you identify with Hodel? Perhaps you also have a difficult decision to make. Do your parents disapprove of some of your behavior or ideas? Do you, like Hodel, think that your parents live by outmoded rules? Is there a serious conflict in your life right now? Search for parallels.

Apply this process to other lyrics. Challenge yourself with a lyric that is difficult for you and hard to identify with. For instance, if you choose "Summertime" (*Porgy and Bess*), a song about mother love, and you have never been a mother, how do you make the connection?

Ask yourself, "What are the qualities associated with motherhood and can I identify with any of them?" Undoubtedly the strongest associations are those of protectiveness, deep caring, and nurturing. Is there someone in your life who you care for in this way? Perhaps it is a friend, a younger brother or sister, or even a pet. In this way, by a process of comparison and substitution, an identification is found.

MEMORY

Memory is involved in almost every human activity. We learn to crawl on all fours and fathom higher mathematics by remembering the progressive steps in the process. We "learn by experience" by remembering the experience—falling off a tree or falling in love—and using it to guide us in future encounters. There are also countless memories that seem to have no purpose at all; yet they enrich our lives through a constant juxtaposition and interplay of past and present, providing us with a context by which to orient ourselves.

The memories of experiences are accumulated in a kind of storehouse of the mind and nervous system. Some of them may lie there forgotten for years until some event spontaneously brings them back to consciousness. Aside from spontaneous recall, purposeful remembering seems to vary a great deal from individual to individual and also within the individual. Some people's memories go back to the earliest childhood; for others, these years are blank. Particular memories are often recalled with ease. Others, especially those associated with negative emotions such as rejection or the loss of a loved one may become deeply buried in the subconscious and be beyond recall.

The use of memory has special applications for the singing actor. Since the portrayal of a character depends to a great extent on the personal qualities that the singing actor is able to project onto the given material, and these personal projections depend in part on the memory of individual experience, there will be a richer portrayal if he can open up the memory and enlarge the amount of available material and information.

Though the memory cannot be fully commanded, it can be prodded and encouraged by means of systematic demands made upon it. One of the best ways of doing this is the following project, which is time-consuming but rewarding.

Exercise

Begin to write the story of your life in the form of an autobiography.[5] For convenience, use a loose-leaf binder.

Going back to the first memories of your childhood, record everything that comes to you. Try not to edit yourself as you go along. Record good, bad, trivial, and significant events without judgment. Encourage the flow of memories by keeping yourself relaxed and open. These pages are not to be shared with anyone; they are your personal journey back into your past.

If certain periods of your life seem to be hazy in your recollection, simply go on to the next; you may be able to fill the gaps in later.

Avoid being merely factual in what you write down. As important as the actual events are the feelings and sensations you experienced along with them. Don't ignore the values that you were exposed to, the moral climate that prevailed in your home, whether your parents were authoritarian or permissive, and so on.

To be most effective, this project should be carried out over a period of several weeks, filling fifty pages or more. The rewards will be

---

[5]For anyone interested in autographical or journal writing, Ira Progoff's *At a Journal Workshop* is highly recommended.

abundant. By reopening the pages of your life, you will bring back to awareness many forgotten memories, thereby increasing your fund of available material in your work as a performer. The self-knowledge that you will gain by making this journey is even more important. You will see patterns of events that have been given a particular direction to your life. You will notice the crossroads where you took one road rather than the other. (What would have changed in your life had you taken the other road?) You will become aware that you struggled with certain issues in your earlier life, and that perhaps some of these are still alive for you and need to be dealt with. Most important, you will obtain an overview of your life and a sense of its uniqueness.

Carry your story right up to the present. If so inclined, continue to record your daily events, thus transforming your autobiography into an on-going journal.

EMOTIONAL RECALL

In the preceding pages memory has been discussed in very general terms. Emotional recall, on the other hand, is a very specific use of memory.

When the imagination alone fails to provide the intensity of emotion that a lyric seems to demand, one way of reaching such a state is to delve into our past history and find an experience that corresponds emotionally to that of the lyric. It does not matter if the particular circumstances of the past experience are quite different, as long as the feelings that dominated the event were similar to those expressed in the lyric.

For instance, in "Just You Wait" (*My Fair Lady*), Eliza, feeling unjustly treated, unappreciated, and humiliated, explodes with anger against Higgins. Applying emotional recall to this lyric, the performer would search for a situation in her past life in which she experienced similar anger and outrage. Perhaps she was once unjustly accused of an offense or stood up for a date.

When the appropriate event has been found, it should be dramatized as if it were happening presently. By means of an improvised monologue, the feelings of anger can be expressed directly at the person who was responsible.

While doing this, it is important that the past event be visualized with all possible richness of detail. Sensory impressions that were associated with the event—colors, sounds, clothing, furnishings—should be vividly recalled.

The performer should also be sensitive to her reactions to these images. Perhaps one small detail will produce a strong surge of feelings. Careful note should be made of this, since such images can be used as catalysts to trigger feelings.

The last step in the process is the application of emotional recall to the song. By transferring the feelings that were real to us to the context of the lyric, an added dimension of "reality" is gained.

Occasionally the performer will choose for emotional recall an incident from life that is so full of emotion that it overwhelms her; she starts crying, loses support of her voice and shows other signs of being out of control. This can happen easily, especially if the theme is lost love or grief over the death of someone close. If the memory is fresh, the impact will be that much greater.

Memories that bring on such extreme reactions obviously cannot be used in performance, since objectivity is lost, and the performer is no longer in charge of herself. A balance between emotion and intellect must always be sought so that the overall objectives of the song or the scene can be achieved. After a suitable lapse of time, it is possible that the same memory can be used for the purpose of emotional recall, provided that control can be maintained.

THE PHYSICALIZATION OF EMOTION

So far we have attempted to show that since we cannot command the emotions, indirect methods of evoking them must be found.

In identification, you think: "I'm like an oak tree in that I'm solid and dependable." This purely mental image will probably cause some slight physical changes to take place spontaneously. Perhaps you'll unconsciously draw your body up and raise your chest. Or maybe you'll set your jaw a little more firmly.

If you are using emotional recall and remembering an incident in your life when you experienced a painful rejection, your body may respond to the memory by a slight collapse of the chest, or you may feel a contraction in the stomach.[6]

These bodily reactions to mental images are due to the fact that, by nature, we are integrated beings, experiencing life in wholes, not fragments; that whatever stimulates one part of our organism finds a correspondence in another. The implication is that if we *allow* ourselves to respond to thoughts and actions in a free and natural way, and if we are not excessively blocked by inhibitions and defenses, we will spontaneously sing with the right vocal sound, make the right facial expression, the right gesture and movement.

This method of inducing emotion can be viewed as proceeding from inside to outside, since it begins with a mental image and results in a physical expression. (The audience, of course, sees only the external reflection of the image.)

There is another equally effective method of inducing emotion that starts at the opposite end, from the outside to the inside. Here we begin with a physical action of some sort—a gesture, posture, or movement—which results in an emotional reaction. The principle underlying this sequence behavior has been formulated by R. Assagioli (1973), who stated: "Attitudes, movements and actions tend to evoke corresponding images and ideas; these, in turn, evoke or intensify corresponding emotions and feelings."[7] Thus, speaking with a harsh voice and behaving as if one is angry tends to awaken real anger. This is often seen in children who begin to fight for fun, but gradually become so involved that they end by fighting in earnest.

That there is an instinctive awareness of this general principle is evidenced by certain common expressions in language, such as "whistling in the dark" (to act as if one were not afraid) or "put on a happy face" (to act happy though feeling sad).

---

[6]Experiments conducted by Dr. Edmund Jacobson using neurovoltmeters to measure muscular activity confirmed the fact that nearly all mental imagery is accompanied by slight, but palpable muscular contractions. See Edmund Jacobson, *Progressive Relaxation* (Chicago: University of Chicago Press, 1938).

[7]R. Assagioli, *The Act of Will* (New York: Viking Press, 1973), p. 52.

To test the efficacy of this idea, try the following simple experiments:

1. Clench your fist hard. Hold it like that for ten seconds. Be aware. Did your jaw also tighten? How about your stomach muscles? What went on in your mind? Did you have any angry thoughts?
2. With eyes closed, gently stroke something soft, like fur or velvet. Do this for half a minute. Allow images and associations to emerge into consciousness. What memories came up? A moment of tenderness experienced in the past? Having comforted someone?
3. Deliberately yawn several times and stretch your body. Note what feelings and images come up.
4. Stand on tip-toes and reach for something high, just beyond your fingertips.
5. Push something away with all your might.
6. Cradle a precious object in your hands.
7. Invent other actions.

Allow yourself to be open and aware in each of these exercises. Take time and don't rush from one action to the next.

Now try the last six experiments again, this time with variations. Each action is to be done in two different ways, according to the descriptive words accompanying it. As before, be sensitive to images and feelings arising out of the actions.

1. Clench your fist hard: a) angrily, b) fearfully.
2. Gently stroke something: a) tenderly, b) sensually.
3. Yawn: a) luxuriously, b) indifferently.
4. Reach for something up high: a) yearningly, b) furtively.
5. Push something away: a) it's disgusting, b) it's dangerous.
6. Cradle a precious object in your hands: a) lovingly, b) greedily.

Note how much more intense each action has become and how much richer the imagery that surfaces as a result of applying an attitude to the action.

The procedure for applying physicalization of emotions to a song is as follows:

First, determine the dominant feeling in the lyric. Next, discover a physical action that characterizes the feeling. This step requires some trial and error to find the most effective action, since we express ourselves in very individual ways. Perform the action while speaking the lyric or that part of the lyric that expresses the particular emotion being evoked. Be very conscious of your body sensations as you do this, since you will want to retain or re-experience them during the actual performance of the song. Finally, perform the song, discarding the action, but keeping alive those inner sensations that the action inspired.

Physicalization

Take the example of "Far From The Home I Love" (see lyrics on page 37). Decide what feeling seems to dominate the song. Suppose you decide it is conflict. You love your father and your family, but your love for your husband is stronger and you must leave your home to be with him.

To be in conflict means to be pulled by opposing forces; to be drawn first to one side, then to the other. How can you express this physically?

One way would be for two people to actually pull you from opposite sides. The one pulling your left arm represents your father and the stronger one pulling your right arm is your husband.

If this is inconvenient, simulate the action; tense your muscles as if you were actually being pulled in opposite directions. Another way would be to pull one hand against the other, as you would in an isometric exercise.

While you are going through the action, think of the words of the song and relate the action to the words. Experience the pain of the conflict; the frustration of knowing that your father will never really understand why you are leaving. In the course of the exercise a powerful feeling may rise in you, and the words may take on a new significance.

Now perform the song while the physical sensation of the conflict is still strong in you. Even though you are now performing alone, you can recall the sensation of being pulled by slightly tensing the particular muscles that were involved in the pulling. If you can let yourself give in to the feelings that want to emerge, you may find yourself suddenly moving and gesturing with a new spontaneity.

Physicalization

In "Something Wonderful" (*The King And I*), Lady Thiang, the King's favorite wife, tried to persuade Anna to see the dying King. She tells her that he is a good man who tries hard, even though he "stumbles and falls."

In the course of the song, Lady Thiang also reveals her own feelings of great love and protectiveness for the King.

What physical actions come to mind when you think of protecting someone you love? Sheltering someone in your arms? Shielding your loved one with outstretched arms, palms back? How would *you* act out the feeling of protectiveness?

Choose one way and, as before, go through the action while thinking or speaking the words. Be aware of emerging feelings and the sensation of physically protecting someone.

Then perform the song, allowing yourself to duplicate the body sensations and feelings that you experienced before.

Physicalization

When Julie in *Carousel* sings "If I Loved You" to Billy Bigelow, she hopes to find out whether Billy feels about her as she does about him. To test him, she spins a little fantasy of what would happen *if* she loved him. It's a charming deception that allows her to stay uncommitted while at the same time drawing him out.

The feeling behind the words and the situation suggest careful balancing, like walking a tightrope. There is the fear of falling, the clutch in the stomach, and the excitement that comes from exposure to danger. All this seems contradicted by the serene melody that accompanies the words, like trying to cover up excitement with an appearance of calm.

Act out walking on a tightrope, hundreds of feet above the ground. Vividly visualize the details. Can you see how small everything looks on the ground? Can you feel the wire swaying under your feet, your balance shifting from second to second?

It is important in these physicalizations to use your imagination to the fullest. The more details you visualize, the better. Try to engage your senses so that you can really see, hear, touch, taste, and smell.

As before, the physical action spurs the imagination which, in turn, activates the emotions. When performing, the sense–memory of the experience is replayed like a tape. The more accurate your recall of the physical sensations, the more easily you'll be able to reuse this memory for future use.

Physicalization

"Everything's Coming Up Roses" (*Gypsy*) is a song of desperate optimism. Momma Rose, crushed because her daughter June has run away, now puts all her hopes of success on Louise, her other daughter. She is determined to make a star of her. In a torrent of frenzied enthusiasm, she tries to convince her daughter that she will make all their dreams come true.

Here are some possibilities for physical actions:

1. Reaching for a prized object and about to succeed in grabbing it.
2. Climbing up a long ladder or stairs. A great reward awaits you at the top. You can do this by climbing an actual staircase, or you can simulate climbing, using pantomimic movement.
3. Opening gift packages. Each one contains a wonderful present. Show your anticipation and joy as you unwrap each one. (Again, you may use actual props to give an added stimulus.)
4. Forcing your way through a surging crowd. They are going in the opposite direction. You struggle through and reach your goal. (A few fellow performers can help you simulate the scene.)
5. You are a magician, capable of the most astounding feats of magic. You have the power to transform any object to whatever you desire. An adoring audience wildly applauds every trick.

"The Impossible Dream" (*Man of La Mancha*) is full of images that lend themselves to physicalization: Fighting an unbeatable foe, reaching an unreachable star, and bearing an unbearable sorrow. Select one that you find particularly meaningful and physicalize it.

In all of the above exercises, try to avoid being self-critical of your movements and gestures. If these seem awkward and unpolished, it doesn't matter for the present; they will become more flowing in time. Remember that the exercise is only a means to an end, and that the actions are not to be used in performance.

For instance, in "Far From The Home I Love," the important thing is keeping the interior sensation of the movement alive while discarding the larger movements. In this particular example, being pulled to and fro is so right for the words that you might allow it to remain visible (very much reduced in scope, of course), especially on the line "Wanting home, wanting him."

Individual exploration of the particular application of the exercise will determine what extent the movements and gestures should be maintained.

The Double Message

One of the differences between animals and humans is the way each displays its feelings. There is never any doubt about how an animal feels. A vicious dog will bare its fangs and lunge at you. A vicious man, on the other hand, might smile in your face and fantasize hitting you when your back is turned. A fearful beast will cower and run away, a fearful human often resorts to bravado to cover up his fear. An affectionate animal will purr and rub against you, a man who feels affection might be incapable of doing more than talk about the weather. We hide and disguise our true feelings in an astounding number of ways.

When we behave in one way and think or feel in a contrary way, the suppressed thoughts and feelings are called the subtext, the text beneath the text.

Disguising the way we think and feel has great dramatic interest because it centers around conflict. On one hand, there is the innate need to respond to stimuli with appropriate feelings, and on the other are the restraints imposed on us by our culture and our particular upbringing that says we must behave not as we think and feel, but according to what others expect of us. As a result of this conflict, we often send out double messages when we communicate.

Message 1 is the words we speak, what we want others to believe, or what we think others expect of us.

Message 2 is what we think or feel. This message is expressed by some kind of body language, eye movements, a tone of voice, or muscular tension or movement in some part of the body.

An important part of this drama of deception is that the person disguising his thoughts or feelings imagines that the disguise is successful. Sometimes it is, but more often it is transparent. The pasted-on smile that covers displeasure is easily recognized, as is the feigned nonchalance that hides a deep hurt. The skill with which the game is played will vary enormously from player to player and in some measure is an indicator of the degree of sophistication of the person.

The individual is not always aware of sending out message 2; especially if it represents an unacceptable feeling. For instance, hostile feelings toward a parent or sibling may be suppressed and felt only as irritation or discomfort. Or a person may unaccountably blush in the presence of another.

On the other hand, the intention of message 1 may be very clearly to cover up, mislead, or deceive.

Two illustrations of the double message in action:

You encounter someone whom you dislike intensely, but because of circumstances, you must be polite. You shake hands, smile, and say, "How are you?" (message 1). This might be accompanied by a slight tightening of the muscles of your face, an edge to your voice, or other body language (message 2). You might also be aware of negative thoughts and your need to control your behavior.

A second example. Again you meet someone. This time you have warm feelings for the other person, but you are shy and embarrassed. You shake hands, smile, and say, "How are you?" (message 1). But now your smile is a little hesitant, your hand is damp, and you have difficulty making eye contact (message 2). All this is, in effect, saying, "I like you very much, but I don't know how to handle that; I'm confused and uncomfortable."

In applying the double message technique to the performance of a song, the first consideration must be whether there *is* an implied counter-meaning behind the words. Very few lyrics actually fall into this category. In the vast majority of cases, when the lyric says "I love you," it means simply that. (An exceptional application will be discussed later.)

However, when a lyric is ambiguous, the singing actor is presented with a challenge that can result in a powerful experience if successfully met.

For example, the language used in "Send in the Clowns" (*A Little Night Music*) is very sophisticated and self-mocking, making light of a situation that is actually terribly painful. We know that it is painful because of the context of the play, by what we read between the lines, and by the character of the music that underscores the text.

The lyric to "I Am My Own Best Friend" (*Chicago*) states, in effect, that experience has taught the singer that it's best not to rely on anyone, that she needs no one, that people are essentially selfish. The point is overstated, and we realize that the words are a defense, that beneath the bravado is a vulnerable ego that doesn't know how else to protect itself.

A far more light-hearted application of the double message occurs in *1776*. Martha Jefferson, toying with Benjamin Franklin and John Adams who are consumed with curiosity about what happened the night before, tells them that although her husband, Thomas, isn't much of a talker, "He plays the violin." She then rhapsodizes on the beauty of his playing, saying that when he is finished she is quite *unstrung*. The subtext is clearly sexual, comparing musical with sexual proficiency. It allows Martha to be charmingly naughty, while at the same time maintaining the ladylike decorum that the period (1776) demanded.

In each of these examples the singer should perform the songs as if to convince someone of the truth of the words. As in real life, when trying to cover up a feeling, we invariably overstate our case, the singer must likewise overstate and exaggerate message 1. The audience then knows that the feelings behind the words are contrary to those expressed. The singer can keep the subtext clear in her mind by consciously thinking "I don't want you (the person to whom she is singing) to know how I feel."

A special application of the double message can be used in certain cases where the lyric contains a potential ambiguity. It consists of taking a

Exercise

Write down or improvise your own message 2 to one of the above songs or another song that fits into this category. Express what you think the unspoken thoughts of the character might be. When you perform the song, let these thoughts dominate your awareness. In other words, *react to the thoughts, not to the words*.

Following is a list of songs that have a strong subtext:

"Barcelona" and "Being Alive" (*Company*)
"Soon" and "You Must Meet My Wife" (*A Little Night Music*)
"Little Lamb" (*Gypsy*)
"At The Ballet" (*A Chorus Line*)
"I Won't Send Roses" (*Mack and Mabel*)
"You've Got To Be Taught" (*South Pacific*)

song with lyrics that have a clear, unequivocal meaning and performing it *as if the words were not true.* The performer, in this instance, creates a subtext for the song by projecting onto it an attitude that is different from the original.

A good example of this technique is Barbra Streisand's version of "Happy Days Are Here Again," one of her earliest recording successes. The original song is a rollicking up-tune, but the Streisand recording becomes a statement of pain and despair. This transformation, interestingly, is accomplished without changing a word of the lyric. The only alteration is that of tempo; it is sung quite slowly. The dramatic metamorphosis results entirely from the new attitude that is imposed on the song. Streisand makes the listener believe that the lyric is a lie; that perhaps the words were once true, but they now bring only pain and anguish. It is a powerful performance.

This method of changing a happy song into a sad one is not new. It derives from opera and operettas and was used with special effectiveness by Oscar Hammerstein and Sigmund Romberg in such works as *New Moon* and *The Student Prince.* Many musicals since then have employed the device as a stock technique. Essentially, it works in this way: In the first act the lovers meet, and boy woos girl with a romantic love song. In the second act, circumstances have separated them. When he or she sings the same song, the words remind them of their former happiness and become a painful memory. (Of course, before the end of the show, they are reunited, and the song is once more a happy one.)

This is what happens in *South Pacific.* Early in the play, Emile De Becque sings "Some Enchanted Evening." In it he expresses his need to find love, and his determination that once he has found it, he will "never let it go." In the second act, the song is reprised. But now everything is changed, and he thinks that he has lost Nellie forever. The same words that once reflected his needs and hopes now become tinged with bitterness and irony. Because of the new circumstances, they carry an entirely new message.

This sort of transformation is most easily realized in the context of a musical, where the performer is lead by the action of the play into new situations. However, the turnaround can also be made to work in a solo appearance if the lyric lends itself to the treatment. Trial and error and audience reaction will determine the success of the transformation.

Let us examine the lyric of "People" (*Funny Girl*)[8] outside the context of the musical for which it was written, determine what the words alone say and imply, and then give it a double message.

Although the entire lyric is written in the third person, the narrator (singer) is certainly referring to herself. It states that human failings like pride, defensiveness, and immaturity keep us from happiness; that in order to be fulfilled in love, people have to allow themselves to need someone. But a person also has to have luck, and luck is either given or not given.

There is also an interesting ambiguity about the lyric. It is never quite clear whether the narrator is one of the lucky ones or not, whether the words are true for her. This gives the performer the option of choosing one of two opposing interpretations.

Let us then use this lyric as a learning in the application of the double message by simultaneously offering two opposite interpretations.

In the table that follows, column one represents Message 1, the original lyric. Column two is Message 2 and is positive. In this version, the assumption is that the narrator is one of the lucky people who has found love. Column three is Message 2 and is negative. Here the assumption is that the words are not true, that the narrator has been disappointed in love. Message 1 is the actual words and music performed by the singer. Messages 2 positive and 2 negative are the thoughts that course through the performer's mind as she sings 1.

The Words As Sung

Message 1: The Lyric	Message 2: The Thoughts (Positive)	Message 2: The Thoughts (Negative)
People, people who need people are the luckiest people in the world.	*I'm* the luckiest person in the world.	People who can say that they need people are the lucky ones. *I'm* sure not one of them.

Message 1: The Lyric	Message 2: The Thoughts (Positive)	Message 2: The Thoughts (Negative)
We're children needing other children and yet, letting our grown-up pride hide all the need inside, acting more like children than children.	I can't imagine how stupid I was, trying to put on this phoney image, hiding my real feelings.	Why is it that this terrible pride can't let me show that I *do* need him? I guess I've never really grown up.
Lovers are very special people; they're the luckiest people in the world.	To think *he loves me!*	Well, I'm special, too. So why can't *I* have love? Why do I have to be alone? It's not fair and it makes me angry.
With one person, one very special person, a feeling deep inside your soul says: you were half, now you're whole.	I feel for the first time that I'm a whole person. Life is going to be so different, so wonderful!	The feeling deep inside me says, "You'll *never* find love. *Never.*"
No more hunger and thirst, but first, be a person who needs people. People who need people are the luckiest people in the world.	It's not hard to say now: I need him. I love him. I'm the luckiest person in the world.	I'm hungering and thirsting and wanting and I'm miserable because I can't let myself go. Damn it all! Why? Why? Why?

The next example demonstrates a sharply contrasting use of this device, showing how varied the results of using contrary meanings can be.

"I Got Rhythm"[9] (*Girl Crazy*) is an extroverted outpouring of joy. What would be the effect if the message of the lyrics was completely ignored, and the song were sung with an attitude of absolute indifference? Let us try it and observe the results.

[9]"I Got Rhythm," by George & Ira Gershwin. ©1930 (Renewed) New World Music Corporation. All Rights Reserved. Used by permission of Warner Bros. Music.

Message 1	Message 2
I got rhythm,	(deadpan expression)
I got music,	
I got my man (girl),	
Who could ask for anything more?	
I got daisies	(absentmindedly scratching face)
In green pastures,	
I got my man (girl),	
Who could ask for anything more?	
Old Man Trouble,	(looking down at feet, toes of one foot
I don't mind him.	start tapping mechanically)
You won't find him	
'Round my door.	
I got starlight,	(suppressing a yawn)
I got sweet dreams,	
I got my man (girl),	(face front, still deadpan)
Who could ask for anything more?	
Who could ask for anything more?	(fading out)

This rather extreme application of the double message is intended to show how flexible this device is. It can be used to express a whole spectrum of thoughts and feelings, from deepest tragedy to the zaniest comedy. The only limits are those that you impose on your own imagination.

Exercise

In the same vein of the preceding example, take any lyric and give it a drastically contrary subtext.

Perform "Almost Like Being In Love" (*Brigadoon*) with an attitude of being highly suspicious.

Perform "My Funny Valentine" (*Babes In Arms*) with an attitude of breaking up with laughter, making fun of him or her.

Perform "The Sound of Music" (*The Sound of Music*) with absolute astonishment and disbelief.

At this point, perhaps we should pause and summarize what has been discussed so far.

To have begun our study of performance in singing/acting with an analysis of lyrics is consistent with the idea that song is a kind of drama;

that the most potent tool a singer has are the words of the text. The words contain the seeds of meaning and emotion that the singer transmits and causes to germinate in his own particular way. Unfortunately, the words are too often the most neglected element in singing. The straight actor willingly accepts the text of the play as his foundation and reads and rereads it in search of more and more particularization of meaning, but the singer frequently relegates the lyrics to a position of secondary importance, often memorizing the words through mechanical repetition. It is not only singers who are guilty of such offenses; many fine actors stop acting the moment they begin to sing. Sometimes, of course, this may be due to an insufficiently developed vocal technique, causing self-consciousness and a consequent tightening of the body. Most often, however, the dissociation of singing and acting results from a careless acceptance of traditional stereotypes that are to be seen every day on stage, film, and television.

Bad acting among singers is virtually a norm, and it becomes natural to conform to the norm. This does not mean that singing cannot be stylized or that movement in association with singing must necessarily be realistic. There is room for all styles of performing for the singing actor—from naturalism to extreme stylization such as in Bob Fosse's work. However, there is a vast difference between expressing oneself in a particular way with intent and thought and the kind of self-indulgent permissiveness that so often goes for singing/acting.

Regarding the various types of lyric analyses, it is not suggested that they necessarily be practiced in the given sequence, but rather applied as the need arises. Some general advice, however, can be given.

Don't learn a song by listening to a recording of it. You will find yourself imitating the phrasing and vocal tricks of the recording artist and killing your own originality. Listening to recordings, of course, is valuable and should be done frequently, but not for the purpose of memorization.

As you are becoming roughly familiar with the words and music of a new song, be sensitive to your first impressions; for instance, a musical or word phrase that brings up a feeling or strong association. Establish what the lyric is trying to say. This includes literal meaning, emotional tone, and intention. A short sentence that captures the essential meaning of the lyric should be kept in the back of the mind like a running theme or motif, and all imagery and metaphoric use of language should be noted and visualized. The lyric should then be retold in the performer's own words. These should be acted out in full, not merely recited.

If the performer has a well-developed imagination and can empathize easily, these devices are usually sufficient to bring his feelings into play. However, if the imagination is uncooperative and needs prodding, the exercises in chapters 5 and 6 will help loosen it up. Through experimentation each performer will find the techniques that are most effective for him.

VOICE
AND DICTION

II

The Speaking Voice

7

We do not learn to speak our native language in school, but at home and in the street. Long before our first day in kindergarten, we have already learned the basic speech patterns that characterize our particular social group. For most of us, the speech we develop by imitating the people in our environment in these early years will stay with us the rest of our lives. Because we learn to speak in such an effortless way and can make ourselves tolerably well understood, we are commonly unaware of our speech habits or the need to train the voice.

The actor, however, needs to be totally aware of the sounds that come out of the mouth and the apparatus that produces the sounds. His mouth, throat, and lungs are to him what the violin is to the violinist. How he expresses himself depends on the control he has of his vocal equipment. Since this book is concerned with singing/acting, the comments on the speaking voice will necessarily be brief. There are many good books on the subject that the reader can refer to.

Following are a list of criteria for good speech. It is of interest to note how many of these correspond to musical criteria. Good speech has the following characteristics:

- It does not attract attention to itself.
- It is clear and understandable, but not overarticulated or stilted.
- It can be easily heard, but is not excessively loud.
- It has variety and expressiveness.
- It is able to reflect the emotions of the speaker.
- It has flow and continuity.
- It does not identify the speaker as coming from a particular region of the country where a particular dialect is spoken. (Unless, of course, the character requires it. Thus, Nathan Detroit in *Guys and Dolls* speaks with a New York Jewish dialect that is appropriate to the play, and Curly in *Oklahoma* reflects the speech of the open West at the turn of the century. This implies that
- Good speech is not necessarily beautiful speech. It is speech that is true to the character and to the situation.

Exercise

Record your voice on a cassette recorder. Select the material from plays or musicals. Listen carefully to what you hear. How does your voice sound in relation to the preceding criteria? Check out each item and notate your comments.

Three fundamental conditions are necessary for good speech: An open throat that is free from tension, sound breathing habits, and the use of optimum pitch level.

In the author's opinion, the great majority of vocal problems in speaking or singing arise from muscular constrictions that prevent the free flow of breath through the throat. The observant eye can see these constrictions in the raising of the larynx, the jutting forward or upward (or both) of the chin, or the visible tension of the neck. The result is a voice that sounds pinched and tight.

The first step in correcting throat tension is to become aware of it. The attention should be focused on the muscles that are active in speaking (or singing) and the quality of the voice checked for stridency or raspiness. A mirror may be used to observe extraneous neck or throat movements of which the individual may be unaware.

If one of these tensions is noted, the next step is to learn to relax the muscles that are involved in the unwanted constrictions. Only the breathing apparatus and the vocal chords are required for the act of phonation. All other muscular clenching contradicts the intention. Following are some relaxation exercises. Their object is to arouse awareness by first exaggerating the tensions and then relaxing the muscles related to the tensions.

Exercise

Head rotation. Slowly rotate your head, taking about six seconds to complete one rotation. As you do this, tense all the muscles of your neck, jaw, and tongue. Do this twice in each direction. While still rotating your head, relax all these muscles and feel the tension leave your neck, jaw, tongue, and throat. Gradually increase the speed of the rotation while at the same time allowing your body to participate in the movement so that the head swings freely.

A variant: Do the same exercise while bending forward, hands resting slightly above your knees. If you are properly relaxed, you should feel the weight of your head as it swings downward, and your jaw should drop down by its own weight.

Jaw tensing. Again rotate your head, but this time keep everything relaxed except the jaw. Be especially aware of your neck muscles and don't allow them to tense. Now relax the jaw and note the difference.

Tongue tensing. Same as above, only this time the tongue is tensed, and everything else is relaxed. Now relax the tongue.

Larynx tensing. Deliberately tense the muscles of the larynx by imagining that you are lifting a heavy weight. Take a deep breath as you would before lifting and note the tension and pressure build up in your larynx. Now relax.

Relaxation through imagery. Search your mind for mental images that you associate with openness, space, and freedom. It might be a grassy meadow in summer, a panorama of wide-spreading mountains, or a tranquil lake. Close your eyes. Let your entire body respond to the image as if you were there. Allow your breathing to become free and effortless. Visualize your throat being as open as that beautiful scene. Now speak some lines from a poem or a play and note whether there is any difference in the sound of your voice, and if it has become more open.

SOUND BREATHING HABITS

Ordinary breathing is an automatically controlled function of the body requiring no intervention by the individual. The amount of air we take into our lungs corresponds to the amount of energy the body is using. During sleep or when we are awake and resting we take in less air than when we exercise or are excited (mental exercise). Our breathing apparatus stokes as much fuel (oxygen) into our furnace as is necessary.

Since in everyday conversation we are in close proximity to our listeners and they are usually familiar with our speech patterns, a minimal increase of air intake is necessary. If we are not heard or understood, we receive feedback that tells us to speak louder or more clearly.

On the other hand, speaking or singing in public requires that breathing be well-developed and efficient. The conditions of public performance may be such that they are adverse to audibility and clarity of speech. For instance, the acoustical environment may be unfavorable, or a large audience may create an undertone of sound that may interfere with audibility. The fact that the performer is usually presenting material that is new and unfamiliar to the audience further adds to the problems of comprehension. Thus, the performer needs to have that extra amount of breath support that will compensate for such conditions. (Clarity of diction is, of course, another key element in communication. More on this subject later.)

The breathing mechanism consists mainly of the diaphragm and the muscles of the chest.

The diaphragm is a large, muscular sheet that separates the abdominal cavity from the chest. When we inhale, this muscle descends, thereby increasing the capacity inside the chest. During exhalation it rises.

The muscles of the chest, especially those of the lower chest, are capable of expanding the ribs so that the chest cavity is enlarged, forcing air into the lungs.

The lungs are two large, cone-shaped organs that fill the chest cavity. The bottom of the lungs, the largest part, contacts the diaphragm. The lungs are passive organs, merely responding to the continual change of air pressure caused by the expansion and contraction of the chest. During expansion, the air pressure inside the chest is lowered, and air rushes in to equalize the pressure. During contraction, the opposite effect takes place.

Although there is some controversy on the subject, most teachers of speech and singing agree that the combined use of diaphragmatic and chest breathing gives optimum results.

The clavicles (collar bones) and shoulders are also a part of the breathing system. However, their use is discouraged because of the tension that is usually caused by raising and lowering the shoulders, and because it is unsightly.

The following exercise demonstrates the combined use of diaphragmatic and chest breathing.

Exercise

Lie on the floor. Place your left hand on your chest, your right hand on your stomach. Breathe in slowly. As you do this, you should first feel your right and then your left hand rising. Be careful not to tense any muscles other than those involved in the act of breathing. Hold the breath for a few seconds. Now exhale slowly through the mouth, holding the chest in a firm position and drawing the stomach slightly in. As the air leaves the lungs, the muscles of the stomach continue to exert a slight upward pressure. During the process note that the contact of your back with the floor increases on inhalation. Relax.

General Hints on Breathing

- Become aware of your breathing habits. Are you a shallow or deep breather? When speaking, do you frequently have to pause for air in the middle of a phrase? Do people say they have trouble hearing you when you speak?
- Good breathing and good posture go together. Avoid both the slouch and the excessively raised chest. Be careful not to jut the chin out or upward. Keep the shoulders dropped.
- Take in just as much air as is needed to last the phrase—neither too much nor too little.
- Learn to breathe quickly and silently. If you are a noisy breather, it means that you are obstructing the breath at the larynx.

THE OPTIMUM PITCH LEVEL

The pitch of a voice is the degree of highness or lowness at which it vibrates. It is determined by such factors as emotional states, age, health, the distance between speaker and listener, and so on. There are individual variations in pitch, just as with any physical attribute. Every voice has a particular part of its range where it sounds best, its quality is most pleasing, and the effort required to produce it is minimal. When a voice is centered around these tones, it is said to be at its optimal pitch level (OPL). Of course, there will be deviations from this center; pitch inflections will rise and fall. This is normal in all speech patterns. But the OPL is the tonal center to which the pitch will gravitate. The following exercises are for finding the OPL.

Exercise

Be sure that your neck, mouth, and throat are relaxed. Stop your ears with your fingers and slowly sing a scale up and down while humming. Listen to yourself carefully and notice at what point in the scale the sound of your voice increases in loudness. Now remove your fingers from your ears and intone the same pitch on the vowel *ah*. This pitch is your optimum pitch level, and your normal speaking voice should center around it. Of course, as your emotional states change, the pitch of your voice will fluctuate accordingly. Thus, in a state of anger or surprise, it will rise, and in a somber mood it will fall.

Variant Exercise

Starting on your lowest comfortable pitch, sing a scale up and down on the vowel *ah*. Listen for a particular note that seems to be louder and more resonant than the others. This is your OPL. Compare this note with the one arrived at in the previous exercise. It should be the same or at least very close in pitch.

EXPRESSIVE SPEECH

We use language not only to impart information to each other, but to convey our attitudes, feelings, and values. When we say that a person speaks expressively, we mean that she reveals something of herself in how she speaks. This is done by:

- Pitching the voice higher or lower.
- Altering the quality or timbre of the voice.
- Varying the loudness.
- Varying the tempo of speech.

Pitch changes can be brought about by either sliding from one pitch level to another or by an abrupt stepping up or down. An example of the sliding kind:

"Oh, you did?" (surprise) Here the pitch slides up.
"Oh, you did." (knowingly) This is a downward slide.

Examples of step-wise shifts in pitch.

"Of course I'll stay. (reassuring) "Of course" will be a step higher than the rest.
"All right, who did it?" (annoyed) "Who did it" will be higher.

Both the slide and the step are used to stress words; however the step is more emphatic and creates a stronger accent.

The quality or timbre of the voice is an indicator of the character of the speaker as well as his emotional state. Thus, the politician or minister, whose profession is convincing people, usually develop voices that are resonant and convincing. By contrast, the person who is a chronic complainer often has a voice that is high and has a pinched quality. Geographical origins can also be detected through voice quality; for instance, the nasality that characterizes the speech of midwesterners or the southern drawl.

Loudness or softness of voice can also indicate character, as does tempo. Hence, the loud-mouthed bully, the mousy, soft-spoken menial, or the frenetic auctioneer.

When we compare expressiveness in speech with that of song, we find some interesting relationships and ambiguities. For example, variations in pitch, which in speech are a way of coloring a phrase and can be optionally applied, are unalterably fixed by the composer in song. Every syllable *must* be sung on a particular pitch. Variations in dynamics—soft or loud—are also specifically indicated, as is tempo, which the printed page may denote with directions such as *slowly, brightly, allegro, andante,* or by metronomic markings: ♩ = 60 and so on. The timbre of the voice may be suggested by some indication such as *darkly* or *without vibrato*. And finally, one finds expression marks relating to the emotional interpretation of a passage. Thus, instructions to sing a passage *sadly* or *angrily*.

At first glance, the comparison of speech with song seems to indicate that the speaker has far more options regarding expressive utterance than does the singer, that he is not bound by the number of restrictions that musical structure demands, and that his palette of colors can be more varied and personal. This is true, but only to a degree.

For example: Although the pitches assigned to the notes of a song are quite definite, the singer can enhance the beauty of a phrase by subtle inflections. Dynamics, tempo, timbre, and emotional expression marks can be personalized to an even greater degree, since these are all relative terms, subject to individual interpretation. The fact is that both speaker and singer *must* go beyond the elementary indications of expression to be found in scripts and songs and use these merely as starting points.

The Singing Voice

8

The ideal singing actor has a well-trained vocal instrument that can do justice to a variety of musical and technical demands. His voice has quality and sustaining power, but it is never used for its own sake; rather, it serves to make the word more expressive and communicating. He is keenly aware of the thoughts and feelings that the song generates; whatever the subject matter of the lyric may be, he strives to connect it with his own existence and reveal something of himself. However, if one compares these rather wishful criteria with what one hears on the stages of musical plays and nightclubs, the question arises whether criteria of any kind exist.

At the far end of this musical spectrum is the singer who has had no vocal training, or worse, just a little. He has difficulty in sustaining long notes, since his breath is insufficiently supported. Vocal climaxes cannot be achieved for the same reason. Generally, the throat muscles are used to force, squeeze, or push the voice out, and the resultant sound reflects this struggle. Working against such vocal limitations, the untrained singer is forced to rely either on sheer energy, or on his expressive talents to put a song across. (There have also been many straight actors like Rex Harrison and Glynis Johns who have been drafted into musicals because they were particularly suited for a role and whose superb acting compensated for any vocal deficiency they may have had.)

At the opposite end of the spectrum is the singer who has had proper vocal training, can produce a good sound in all registers, enunciates words clearly, but nevertheless fails to interest his audience. A stereotyped sameness often characterizes the performance of such singers; vowels are uniformly sustained in order to create a continuous sound; consonants are sharply clipped with predictable consistency; and vibrato is applied to every sustained note, regardless of the feeling content of the phrase. Attention is given primarily to vocal production with the consequent neglect of interpretive values. A foreigner with no knowledge of the English language would find it difficult to distinguish whether such a singer were singing of joy or sorrow.

The middle section of the spectrum is composed of performers who, in varying degrees, combine the skills that are associated with the musical theater and nightclubs. Thus, there are singing actors, acting singers, and singing dancers.

While public acceptance for such a wide diversity of vocal quality has allowed many performers who are better actors than they are singers to appear on the musical theater stage, it has also encouraged performers who sing on the level of Rex Harrison, but who have neither his acting ability nor his charisma to seek careers in this field.

Taking into consideration both the diversity of talents and the eclecticism of writing that exists today in the musical theater and popular music—a diversity that makes it impossible to name any one performance style preeminent—let us nonetheless offer some guidelines for the student performer. These are based on a respect for the melody and text of the song and the belief that truth in performance can be both interesting and entertaining.

THE "RIGHT" VOCAL SOUND

The "right" vocal sound is the sound that is appropriate for the mood and feeling of the lyric and for the character who sings them. It sounds "right" because it fits the words and is congruent with the meaning expressed by them. Both words and sound "say" the same things.

Congruency will occur in the most natural manner if it is allowed to happen and is not interfered with. For instance, in ordinary speech we convey what we mean not only by the content of the words we use but by the quality of our voices. Thus, when we feel angry, our voices have a harsh sound, and when we feel loving and tender, our voices become soft and gentle. On the other hand, if someone said "I love you" with a harsh tone of voice, you would probably experience confusion or disbelief. And if you were told "I hate you, go away" in a soft, gentle tone of voice, you would be thrown off balance by the incongruity. In ordinary human intercourse we are very aware of congruence and use it as a means of judging sincerity and genuineness. We are also quick to detect discrepancies that might be clues for ulterior motives.

It is curious that singers, who, like other individuals, are quite aware of this need for congruence in their everyday lives, often lose this awareness the moment they begin to sing. Hence, it is not unusual to hear a love song rendered with a vocal sound that belongs to a robust outdoor song or a joyous song that sounds solemn. The singer who is guilty of such inconsistency is not concerned with the truth of his performance, but with the opulence of his voice. He has come to like and accept a certain vocal quality in himself. That quality then becomes "his" sound, his self-identification. He has typed himself into a particular mode of vocal expression.

Exercise

Pick a song that you know well. Study all the elements that have been considered up to this point, paying particular attention to emotional content.

Record the song on a cassette recorder and carefully listen to the playback in terms of congruence. For instance, if you decide in your analysis that the feeling at the beginning of the song was one of loneliness, does the quality of your voice depict that loneliness? If not, why not? What *does* your voice project? Rerecord the song and try to make your voice say "I'm lonely."

If the mood changes to one of hope later in the song (as, for instance, in "Who Can I Turn To"), listen again and judge whether your voice reflects the new feeling. Rerecord the song as often as necessary to achieve the congruence of feeling and sound.

LEGITIMATE VERSUS POP SOUND
IN MUSICAL THEATER

The kind of vocal sound required of a performer, whether legitimate or pop, also depends on the musical style of the particular show.

Musicals can be roughly divided into two broad categories: Category one, the so-called conventional musical, is typified by the works of Rodgers and Hammerstein or Lerner and Loewe. These works follow a line of musical evolution that began in Europe with the operettas of Johann Strauss (*Die Fledermaus*), Franz Lehar (*The Merry Widow*), Jacques Offenbach (*Orpheus in the Underworld*), and others. Transplanted to America, operettas flourished in the works of Victor Herbert (*Babes in Toyland*), Rudolph Friml (*Rosemarie*), and Sigmund Romberg (*The Student Prince*). They were further transmuted and Americanized by such composers as Jerome Kern and Vincent Youmans during the 1920s and 1930s.

Several landmark musical plays, *Show Boat* (Kern and Hammerstein), *Pal Joey* (Rodgers and Hart), and *Oklahoma* (Rodgers and Hammerstein) abandoned the then prevailing concept that musicals were primarily entertainment and opened up the era of the integrated musical.[1] Instead of having music and choreography superimposed over a flimsy plot, in the newer vision all the elements were skillfully related to one another in a cohesive manner, and unity of concept became an ideal.

These changes in concepts notwithstanding, vocal writing in the conventional musical has continued to be based on classical traditions and consequently requires singers with "legitimate" vocal training.

The second category of musicals rejects the primarily European background of the first and expresses itself in more indigenous ways. Its major influences are the music of Black America—the blues, spirituals and ragtime—as developed by composers such as George Gershwin, Duke Ellington, Harold Arlen, and others. During the 1950s the phenomenon of rock music took over the field of popular music and eventually invaded musical theater with *Hair* (1967). Note the variety of influences in the following shows:

---

[1]*The American Musical Theater* by Lehman Engel is recommended for those readers who have an interest in the history and the structure of musicals.

A Chorus Line	Contemporary rock
West Side Story	Bernstein's own mixture of jazz and contemporary classical music styles
Hair	Late 1960s rock
Grease	A spoof on the rock music of the 1950s
Ain't Misbehavin'	Early 1940s jazz
The Wiz	Soft to hard rock

Each of these shows is written in a musical language as distinct as the speech of a television anchor man is from street language. Some, like *A Chorus Line,* represent current musical trends. Others, like *Grease,* are expressions of a past era and constitute musical nostalgia.

The performer auditioning for one of these shows, is expected to understand that particular musical idiom and be able to sing in its style with ease and naturalness. Freedom of phrasing and interpretation is not only allowed, but encouraged, since the performer's individual musical creativity is valued. (This applies mostly to the last four shows mentioned above.)

It is relevant at this point to mention the female *belting sound.* This is a loud, driving sound that is produced by pushing the natural chest register beyond its normal limits. Most "belters" can carry it fairly comfortably up to around a B♭ in the middle of the staff. Beyond this point it is apt to sound strained, and the voice is in danger of cracking. This quality of sound has been identified with certain roles like Annie in *Annie Get Your Gun,* Babe in *Pajama Game,* Ado Annie in *Oklahoma,* or any of the roles performed by Ethel Merman, Carol Burnett, Carol Channing, Gwen Verdon, and Chita Rivera.

Inexperienced performers, not knowing how to use the belting sound properly and concerned only with getting a big sound, often seriously injure their voices, sometimes beyond repair. Under the guidance of a good voice teacher who is willing to work with this problem (not many will wish to), the belting sound can be learned to be used without impairing the voice. Listening to such artists as Barbra Streisand, Joni Mitchell, Edie Gorme and Linda Ronstadt, one can hear that the chest voice, as it rises up the scale to around G or A in the middle of the staff, becomes blended with the head voice. Ideally, the blend should be such that the change-over is imperceptible. Before this becomes possible, however, the head voice needs to be developed sufficiently to make the smooth connection from one register to the other possible. Many young female performers resist developing the head voice, thinking that it makes them sound "legit." This is not true. The head voice or any other register can be made to sound appropriate if the right preparation has gone into the song. Besides, the alternatives are either to limit oneself to a small range or risk serious injury by forcing the belting voice too high.

A NEEDLESS CONFLICT:
A DIGRESSION

It is unfortunate that an attitude of antipathy is often encountered between so-called legitimate and popular singers. There is a great deal of snobbery in both camps, along with an unwillingness to accept the values and esthetic concepts of the opposing side. The popular singer ridicules the acting of the opera singer, who, in turn, deprecates the vocal crudities of the popular singer. Actually, the best performers in either camp have a great deal in common, and their esthetic criteria are likely to be very similar.

Both the legitimate and the popular singer need to have technical command over their vocal apparatus; both are primarily concerned with human values and the expression of those values and try to communicate to the listener the unique, personal thoughts and feelings that the song evokes in them.

There *are* differences, of course. One of them centers around the relative difficulties of the respective literatures. It obviously takes a great deal more vocal training to sing "Un Bel Di" or "Largo Al Factotum" than "Oh, What a Beautiful Mornin'." The concert singer must endure years of rigorous training in order to develop the range and quality of voice to enable her to sing the literature. No doubt, with many singers the intensity and preoccupation with vocal training, the constant evaluating and listening to the sound of the voice, and the striving for incredibly high vocal standards tends to depersonalize the voice and give it an abstract, stereotyped sound. Such a sound may conform to pedagogic criteria, but it may also lose the human qualities that go to the heart of the listener. The true artist knows that in the end she must make technique subservient to music and feeling, and that the voice must adapt itself from moment to moment to the demands of the text. The presence of so many outstanding opera singers who superbly combine technique with musicality is ample proof that this is possible.

The singer in musical theater, by comparison, is faced with far less rigorous vocal requirements. However, she must adapt herself to many different styles of singing, running the gamut from legitimate to jazz to hard rock. Versatility becomes an important asset, since it has a direct relationship to employability.

In nightclubs and pop concerts, even fewer vocal demands are made on the singer; she more or less sets her own criteria. She can choose to avoid any technical problems that come up. If the vocal range is too high for the singer, a lower key can be chosen; if, as a result, some of the low notes become inaudible, substitute notes can be found, and so forth. In such a permissive atmosphere, there is the temptation for the performer to indulge herself, to take the line of least resistance.

This is the attitude of those who fall by the wayside. Popular singers who achieve success invariably are those who work hard and take performing very seriously. Aside from technical studies, they learn by listening not only to the best singers in their field, but to the great instrumentalists as well. Ella Fitzgerald's debt to the outstanding jazz players of the swing and bebop eras is well known, as is Frank Sinatra's tribute to Tommy Dorsey.

VOCAL PROJECTION

Projecting the voice implies a reaching out toward the listener. The primary factor is the distance between the singer and the listener. The greater the distance, the greater the need to throw the voice. Legitimate vocal training puts great stress on vocal projection, since one of its aims is to equip the singer with enough vocal power to cover the vast distances between an opera or concert stage and the farthest reaches of the house. The singer is trained under conditions of natural acoustics. This constitutes one of the chief differences between the legitimate and the popular singer, since the latter *always* has the microphone at his disposal.

Total amplification of sound has become the norm for every theater, nightclub, pop concert, and other live musical media. With it, traditional concepts of vocal projection have been necessarily altered. Since the microphone enables the weakest voice to become as audible as the strongest, the only reason to sing with force is to achieve intensity of sound.

Furthermore, even some opera houses today use what is euphemistically called "sound enhancement" (partial amplification) in order to achieve a more even spread of sound throughout the house. When recordings, television, and films are added to the list, a picture emerges of a world that is, for better or worse, almost totally amplified.

As important as the microphone's power to equalize voices in terms of projection is its ability to change the quality of sound. With the growing sophistication of audio equipment, even relatively inexpensive systems have electronic equalizers, limiters, and reverb. These sound modifiers can substantially alter the quality of the voice. There is no doubt that these devices are here to stay and will increase in sophistication and in use in the coming years. More and more compact sound systems are becoming available to musicians and singers, and experiments in sound modification will surely continue.

All this considered, it certainly behooves the singer of today to acquaint himself with the world of audio and to find ways and means of practicing with audio equipment. (These comments apply to singers in nightclubs and pop concerts primarily. The standard amplification in musicals is by foot mikes, shotgun mikes, and body mikes. The singer has no control of these, since the levels are set by an audio technician.)

First, he must learn how to physically handle a mike. This is mostly a matter of familiarity: learning how near to hold the mike for the best quality of sound; learning how to hold it in an attractive manner; and learning not to overenunciate plosive sounds, especially *p*'s and *t*'s.

It would also be advantageous to experiment with the various ways of modifying the quality of the voice electronically, to note what happens to the voice when the bottom frequencies are cut out, when the middle range is boosted, and so on.[2]

INTIMACY
VERSUS FORMALITY

In addition to eliminating the problem of projection and making modifications of vocal quality possible, the microphone has also influenced the singer-audience relationship. Through the immediacy of sound, it has

---

[2]See David Bird, *From Score to Tape* (Boston: Berklee Press Publishers, 1973) for a demonstration of the recording process. (The book includes a record.)

allowed the singer to come in close contact with his audience and establish an intimacy that had not been possible before, certainly not with large audiences. By not having to force his voice, the singer can immeasurably increase his palette of vocal nuances so that the slightest inflection and the most minute accents can be registered.[3] Whispered sounds, sibilant sounds, and especially the sounds of breathing create a feeling of great contact between singer and listener. It is this illusion of intimacy that makes it possible for every member of an audience to feel personally addressed and may, in part, account for the extreme idolization of performers that has been such a phenomenon in our time.

Intimacy and expressiveness, however, are certainly not the exclusive domain of the popular singer. In the concert and opera fields, there are such superb artists as Magda Oliveira, Renata Scotto, Dietrich Fischer-Dieskau, Luciano Pavarotti, Italo Tajo, and Tito Gobbi, all of them singing actors of the highest caliber, capable of expressing the full range of human experience.

Unfortunately, they are far outnumbered by those singers who have become locked into stereotypical molds. A preoccupation with voice for the sake of voice characterizes such singers, as does a somewhat stiff attitude toward the audience. That they most often sing in foreign languages (usually imperfectly mastered) further adds to the artificiality of their performance.

It is hardly any wonder that when the legitimate singer ventures into the field of musical theater and is asked to become more "real" and believable, he often experiences serious difficulties. On the other hand, the popular singer sometimes only differs from his legitimate brother in the nature of his stereotypes; he is often similarly bound and immobilized by attitudes that he unquestioningly clings to. The most prevalent of these is that in order to be a "personality" he must always be identifiable, hence, always the same.

This is the point of departure for the singing actor from both the legitimate singer and the "personality" singer. The singing actor must constantly renew himself, discarding old roles or interpretations, creating new ones, never mechanically repeating himself, always discovering and revealing his own uniqueness. Certainly, his personality and life history

---

[3]M. Feldenkrais has observed that discrimination is finest when the stimulus is smallest. This implies that the audience can differentiate between *pp* and *ppp* more easily than *ff* and *fff*.

help him to shape and color his interpretations, but he does not use these to fix himself into a rigid character type that has the quality of predictability. He minimizes his idiosyncrasies rather than indulging them.

For the singer who has had primarily legitimate training and wants to understand and develop a feeling for the popular music of today, the following suggestions may be of help:

- Learn to sing the words rather than the music.
- Practice reading the words out loud so you can get a natural feeling for them.
- Never make a vocal sound for its own sake. Let the sound serve the word, not the other way around.
- Allow yourself the freedom to play with the musical phrase. Sing with rubato.
- Be in contact with your audience. *Share* your song with them; don't sing *at* them.
- Become aware of your body. Are there parts of it that are rigid and unyielding? Try to relax these areas.
- Even while singing in a large hall, imagine yourself in intimate surroundings, singing for a few good friends.

PARLANDO SINGING

Parlando (from the Italian, meaning speaking) singing is a form of vocal expression that falls somewhere between speaking and singing. Although the pitch and rhythm of the melody are generally observed in this style of singing, the tone quality of the voice approaches that of natural speech. This is effected by (1) shortening the notes (nonlegato singing), since this is one of the characteristics of speech, and (2) by singing the pitches of the notes in a way that corresponds to the inflections of ordinary speech. The ends of phrases are often inflected downward, one of the distinctive traits of the English language.

The degree of application of the parlando style depends on the nature of the material and the intentions of the singer. It can be applied to an entire song or a single word; it is equally effective for a highly emotional passage or for one that is broadly comical.

In parlando singing the melody is sung nonexpressively, therefore the words are brought into sharper relief, enhancing diction and comprehensibility. This is particularly desirable in fast patter songs or wordy narrative songs.

1. "The Love of My Life" *(Brigadoon):* This song consists of twelve verses of narrative, full of proper names and comic lines, all done at a good clip, requiring the sharpest diction. It can only be effective by eliminating all expressiveness from the melody and concentrating exclusively on the narrative. Another example from the same show with an even faster tempo is "My Mother's Wedding Day."

2. "When I'm Not Near the Girl I Love" *(Finian's Rainbow):* Sung by a leprechaun, this song is full of the most delightful and outrageous humor and would sound ludicrous if sung with legitimate vocal production.

3. "You Can't Get a Man With a Gun" *(Annie Get Your Gun):* The Western locale of the song, the down-home character of Annie, and the many jokes in the lyrics make the song a natural for this kind of singing.

Because of vocal limitations, there are performers who have been forced to adopt the parlando style of singing as their usual mode of expression. In some cases (Rex Harrison in "My Fair Lady," for instance) the results were so felicitous that other performers with far better voices than Mr. Harrison adopted his manner of singing the part.

The late Maurice Chevalier made the parlando style his trademark. He *never* really sang a song in any vocal sense; it was always half spoken and half sung. Although no doubt he was forced into this style by his vocal deficiencies, it worked superbly for him.

Another application of this style of singing is in the verses of songs. Verses, by their nature, are introductory, setting up the story situation that will lead to the main body of the song, the chorus. They are also often conversational in character, lending themselves to a talking delivery. For example, in "A Foggy Day," the verse begins casually with

> I was a stranger in the city.
> Out of town were the people I knew.[4]

The parlando voice would be appropriate for this mood. Later, the chorus of the song begins,

> A foggy day in London Town.
> Had me low and had me down.

---

[4] *"A Foggy Day,"* by George Gershwin & Ira Gershwin. Copyright ©1937 by Gershwin Publishing Corp. Copyright Renewed, Assigned to Chappell & Co., Inc. International Copyright Secured. ALL RIGHTS RESERVED. Used by permission.

A fuller, more expressive sound can be employed here. In this way, musical contrast is effected between verse and chorus, and a sense of their relative importance is established.

Going one step further than parlando singing, there are moments in song when the most fitting thing to do is to abandon singing pitch altogether and to simply *speak*. Several objectives are gained by doing this: (1) the particular word or phrase that is spoken is, in effect, brought into relief, and (2) a quality of realism is added to the word or phrase, since spoken words are a more natural form of expression than words that are sung.

The literature of both opera and musical theater is full of examples of passages that are to be spoken. Sometimes, as in "I Wonder What the King Is Doing Tonight" *(Camelot)* or "All Er Nothin' " *(Oklahoma)*, whole sections of lyrics are indicated in this way. Elsewhere, single words or phrases are contrasted in this manner.

Aside from such printed instructions, the singing actor can use his own sense of appropriateness to determine precisely where to employ a spoken word in the midst of melody.

If the song is one that is highly emotional, as, for instance, "The Party's Over" *(Bells Are Ringing)*, there is often a flooding of feeling at one point, causing a choking of the voice. This rush of emotion pinpoints the moment at which a word or two can be spoken rather than sung. Thus:

> Now you must wake up.
> All dreams must end.
> Take off your make-up.
> The party's over.
> It's *all over*, my friend.[5]

(In this case the italicized words might be spoken with telling effect.)

In studying the performances of the best singing actors, the student performer should pay careful attention to the use of the parlando sound. It should be distinguished whether the voice is being used expressively or nonexpressively; whether there are slight deviations from the true pitch of a note (intentional deviations, of course); and whether any words or phrases are actually spoken. It then should be determined what has been gained by using this style. Has a special mood been created? Is the line funnier, more emotional, or natural for having been sung (spoken) in this way? The performer is encouraged to apply this technique to various songs and to find the fitting moment for its use.

PHRASING IN SINGING

If we consider a song to be the expression of a complete musical and literary idea, then each section of the song contributes to the development of that idea. In a conventional thirty-two bar song the usual division is by eight bars. The great majority of songs are constructed according to AABA and less often ABAB. These eight-bar sections are then broken down into smaller segments called *phrases*.

A phrase is a group of related notes, usually two or four bars in length, that conveys a musical thought or unit. Like a phrase in a sentence, a musical phrase is usually incomplete by itself and needs other phrases to complement or balance it. Similarly, the end of a phrase in both words and music is most often followed by a pause, which allows time for a breath. Breathing and phrasing are closely connected, since the amount of air taken must be sufficient to last out the phrase.

In songs that are well written, the musical phrases and those of the sentence structure coincide so that the breathing pauses make musical as well as grammatical sense. When they do not, the performer should give preference to the element he considers the most important at the moment.

Some general suggestions are as follows:

- Don't breathe in the middle of a phrase if it can be helped. *Never* breathe in the middle of a word.
- Punctuation is phrasing. Breathe after a comma, semicolon, colon, or period. (A review of the section on punctuation in Chapter 2 is recommended.)
- Be aware of the *entire* sentence and the *entire* musical phrase before making decisions regarding breath pauses.
- If a breath must be taken in the middle of a phrase, either minimize the time it takes to breathe, or try to justify the breath (find a dramatic reason).

Examples

In the following song, the check marks indicate where a breath could be taken.

(1) Somewhere over the rainbow, (✓)
Way up high, ✓
There's a land that I heard of
Once (✓) in a lullaby. ✓

(5) Somewhere over the rainbow, (✓)
Skies are blue, ✓
And the dreams that you dared to dream (✓)
Really do come true. ✓

(9) Someday I'll wish upon a star, ✓
And wake up where the clouds are far
Behind me, ✓
Where troubles melt like lemon drops, ✓
Away above the chimney tops, ✓
That's where you'll find me. ✓

(15) Somewhere over the rainbow, ✓
Blue-birds fly. ✓
Birds fly over the rainbow, (✓)
Why then, oh why can't I? ✓
(four-measure interlude)
If happy little blue-birds fly beyond the rainbow, ✓
Why, oh why (✓) can't I?[6]

If possible, the first two lines should be sung on one breath, as should the next two. However, if the vocal development is inadequate to carry the breath that far, the compromise breath marks (✓) may be observed. The breath marks for the rest of the lyric are based either on punctuation or common sense. Reading the lyric by itself and trying out various phrasings, the correct breathing pause will usually be quite obvious.

The last breath, before *can't I?* is a necessary compromise. It doesn't make lyrical sense, but it is needed to provide enough air for the last long note of the song. (Generally, the ending notes of songs most often require this kind of concession.)

Also note the four-bar interlude before the last line. Here is an opportunity to fill these lines with relevant thoughts that will carry you into the last line. Create a mental soliloquy to bridge the two lines.

"If I Loved You" *(Carousel)* (lyric on page 16) is written in long four-bar phrases which should, ideally, be sung in one breath. If, however, a breath has to be taken, it should be minimized so that the melodic line is as sustained as possible.

The first two lines comprise the beginning phrase, line three being the balancing phrase that completes both the musical and lyrical thought. If a breath is unavoidable at the end of the second line (after the word *say*), it should be done unobtrusively. Most important, the *thought* of the whole sentence must be kept alive.

The middle section of the song begins with line seven. If the punctuation is carefully observed, the breathing places will be natural and musical. A common error often committed in this section is to take a breath after *golden chances* in order to have enough power to sing the climactic notes on *pass me by*. This is a poor choice, since the meaning of the sentence as well as the musical flow will suffer.

At the end of line eleven, the singer has the option of either taking a breath or singing lines eleven and twelve in one breath. The latter choice is definitely preferred, especially if a crescendo is effected as the word *go* is blended into *longin'*. A wonderful sense of urgency results from carrying the voice across the phrase.

Good musical phrasing is no esoteric mystery. It results when common sense is applied to language and music, and when the performer thinks in complete thoughts rather than in individual words or notes. When problems of breathing capacity and vocal strength arise, satisfactory solutions can nevertheless be found, provided that the larger objectives (meanings) are kept foremost.

Instrumentalists, incidentally, often provide excellent examples of good phrasing that singers can emulate. Henry Pleasants in his book, *The Great American Popular Singers,* quotes Frank Sinatra paying high tribute to Tommy Dorsey.

> The thing that influenced me most was the way Tommy . . . . would take a musical phrase and play it all the way through without breathing, for eight, ten, maybe sixteen bars. . . . Fascinated, I began to listen to other soloists. I bought every Jascha Heifetz record I could

find, and listened to him play hour after hour. His constant bowing, where you never heard a break, carried the melody line straight on through, just like Dorsey's trombone. It was my idea to make my voice work the same way as a trombone or violin—not sounding like them, but "playing" the voice like those instruments. . . .[7]

THE VIBRATO

Vibrato is the steady pulsation of the voice that is heard on a sustained note. The pulsation is caused by a slight fluctuation in pitch above and below the tonal center of the note.

The norms for vibrato are difficult to define, since they vary greatly, not only from one musical style to another, but from singer to singer.

With folk singers Joan Baez and John Denver, for instance, the vibrato is so fast that it can no longer be called such; it is, rather, a tremolo—a rapid trembling of the pitch. On the other hand, in rock music as well as jazz, one finds every possible kind of vibrato, both as to the speed of pulsation and amplitude of pitch fluctuation. Vibrato*less* singing has also become quite acceptable since the advent of rock music. James Taylor, whose style falls somewhere between rock, jazz, and folk, is an example of a singer who often uses practically no vibrato, yet sings with a haunting expressiveness. The delicate timbre of his voice and his ability to understate feelings create a musical quality that is uniquely his. He also makes effective use of subtle accents and glides to color his phrasing, all with minimal use of vibrato.

Barbra Streisand, by contrast, uses vibrato with singular discretion and effectiveness. She will frequently sing with a straight tone until the moment comes for a particular stress on a word or at an emotional peak. When the vibrato is brought to bear at such a moment, it has immeasurably greater expressiveness for having been restrained. For example, in her recording of "What Are You Doing The Rest Of Your Life?" (Columbia Records), the title line is sung slowly with a straight tone, and the vibrato is gradually introduced on the word *life*. For the next sixteen measures the vibrato is used very sparingly to give a slight emotional stress to particular words such as *all, me* and "*deep* in your eyes."

[7]Henry Pleasants, *The Great American Popular Singers*, pp. 192–193.

The release (middle section) of the song has a more agitated feeling and brings the vibrato into fuller and more consistent use. At the very end of the song, the upward octave leap on the words *with you* is again rendered with a straight tone, pianissimo and is a lovely ending.

It is only in legitimate singing that the following consistent criteria regarding vibrato can be said to exist. A normal vibrato should pulsate at a rate of six to seven times per second. The fluctuation of pitch up and down from the tonal center of the note should not exceed a semitone. With the exception of parlando passages and certain comic effects, vibrato should be applied consistently to every note. (These general rules are, of course, not to be applied pedantically, but with discrimination and a sensitivity for the desired musical goals.)

The singing actor, whether in opera, musical theater, or nightclubs, needs to be aware of the expressive power of the vibrato and of the variety of its uses. First of all, it should not attract attention to itself, but sound so natural that the listener is completely unaware of it, hearing only the message of the words and music. Again, congruence is all-important. Thus, if a song depicts strong emotions, an intense vibrato may be appropriate. If the mood is languid and serene, the vibrato should, in turn, reflect these qualities (a vibrato with a moderate pulsation rate and a small pitch amplitude would be appropriate). In a comedy song, on the other hand, the use of vibrato is out of place, and a straight tone would help bring out the comic qualities of the song. Paradoxically, the use of the straight tone can also achieve the very opposite effect of the one just mentioned. It can create an atmosphere of extreme fear or unreality as, for instance, in "Mama, Look Sharp" *(1776),* in which the singer describes a boy who has been killed in a skirmish and imagines him trying desperately to communicate with his mother, who is looking for him.

A particular use of vibrato is to heighten the climactic effect of long notes. This is a device used by many popular singers. If it is not overdone, it can be useful. Its application is usually near the end of a song during the sustaining of a long note. The note is begun with a straight tone, and the vibrato is gradually introduced with more and more intensity. The effect is one of great excitement and finality.

Intelligently and expressively used, vibrato is one of the most important means of communicating moods and feelings that the singer has. When it is uncontrolled, as in a slow wobble or a fast tremolo, it can ruin an otherwise good voice. Unfortunately, insufficient attention is paid to vibrato in vocal training. A good vibrato is supposed to happen naturally if all the other conditions of voice production are right. This is no doubt true, but it does not help the singer who has a problem vibrato.

Often a singer is so used to the sound of his own vibrato that he has no objective way to judge himself. Listening to his voice on cassettes can help gain some objectivity, as can listening to singers who do not have this problem. Sometimes, for the sake of exploring unsuspected qualities in one's own voice, imitating the voice qualities of various singers can be a fruitful and surprising experience. In fact, it is not uncommon for the imitation to have qualities of sound that are superior to the singer's "natural" sound.

DICTION

One of the most troublesome problems that the performer in a musical play faces is making the transition from speech to song in a way that does not attract attention to itself. Ideally, the blending of one into the other should hardly be perceptible, so that singing sounds like an extension of speech, and vice versa. In actuality, however, on hearing the first notes of a song, the listener often experiences an unpleasant, jarring sensation resembling the abrupt shifting of gears while driving. When this happens, the concentration of the audience is interrupted, as is the flow of the play. There are several causes for this effect.

For one thing, the performer makes no effort to blend the volume of his speaking voice with that of his singing voice. Consequently, when he starts to sing, he suddenly sounds louder.

Furthermore, his posture changes radically. As the actor, he looked natural and believable; as the singer, he looks puffed up and artificial.

Finally, his diction takes on a transformation. As the actor, he pronounced his words to conform with the character he is playing; as the singer, he pronounces them in a stereotypical way that is out of character.

It seems superfluous to say that such incongruities should be avoided, for they destroy whatever theatrical illusion has been created, not to mention that they are illogical and unthinking.

Unless there is some valid justification to the contrary, a song emerging from a scene should start at the same level of volume as the dialogue that precedes it. One way of effecting a smooth transition from speech to song is for the performer to speak or partially speak the first line of the song. The same kind of transition should apply to the emotional elements; there should be no abrupt shifts. It makes absolutely no sense to go from dialogue that expresses itself in mild emotional tones into a song of white-hot passion.

Posture and movement should similarly express continuity. However, if the musical number is to be staged in a choreographic manner, the mode of expression is no longer that of realism, but rather of a particular style of movement, and the consistency with that style then becomes a criterion.

The Goals of Singing Diction

- The smooth connection of words so that the melodic line can be sustained to the fullest.
- Clarity of pronunciation so that the meaning of the lyric is easily understood.
- The communication of the emotional message behind the words.
- The reflection of the origin and/or education of the character.

A sustained melodic line is achieved by singing mainly on the vowels. It is not the slighting of consonants, but the minimizing of their time values together with a maximizing of the time values of vowels that produce the effect of a continuous sound. To fully focus the attention on the vowels, it is a useful exercise to sing a phrase of a song eliminating consonants altogether and singing only on vowels. The dramatic effect this treatment has on the quality of the voice is quite astonishing. The exercise tends to open the voice and allow the sound to emerge more freely. Try, for instance, to sing the first four notes of "If I Loved You" using only vowels. Thus:

If I loved you

I – AH(i) – UH – OO

(The *(i)* in the second sound is the tail-end of the diphthong of *I* and should be delayed and then quickly connected to the next vowel.)

Clarity of diction and comprehensibility obviously go hand in hand. Can the audience understand you when you speak or sing? Can they understand you without straining or guessing? There is nothing that will irritate an audience more than to have to do this.

The performer needs to constantly keep in mind that the words he speaks or sings (with the exception of repertory pieces) are being heard for the first time, and that all sorts of acoustical impediments (not to mention the distance between performer and audience) add to the problems of comprehensibility.

Often a song will contain a line that is repeated three or four times during the course of the song. It is the *first* time the line is sung that it needs to be enunciated most clearly.

Some sentence structures are more difficult to understand at first hearing than others. Sometimes two sequential words that could be easily understood if spoken, will be difficult to differentiate when run together in song.

There are also physiological factors beyond the control of the individual that affect diction. The act of speaking involves an astonishing number of anatomical parts that must join in efficient, cooperative functioning in order to produce clear speech. Jaw, teeth, lips, tongue, soft and hard palate, mouth conformation, and numerous other parts each have a specific function in determining the quality and characteristics of the words we say or sing. Clear speech is a talent that has nothing to do with education. We constantly observe people who have no speech training but speak with great distinctiveness, and others with the advantage of training who have problems.

When there are physical factors that cause poor speech patterning, some form of speech therapy may be necessary. However, aside from such cases, poor diction is most usually the result of slovenly speech habits acquired early in life and never corrected. If we have poor models to imitate in our formative years, we perpetuate their mistakes. The necessary recourse is to embark upon a rigorous period of specialized training, which is not within the scope of this book.

We now come to specific ways of dividing syllables in song. The common division that one sees in printed music will not do, since, by custom, it is based on dictionary syllabication and will not help the singer achieve a sustained vocal sound. This can only be effected by singing on the vowels—that is, by maximizing the duration of the vowels so that they blend into one another with a minimum of interruption by consonants. A comparison of the printed with the altered syllabication will illustrate the difference.

Dividing the Syllables

The original lyric of "Oh, What a Beautiful Morning' " *(Oklahoma),* as it appears in the printed vocal score, is as follows:

> Oh, what a beau-ti-ful morn-in',
> Oh, what a beau-ti-ful day,
> I got a beau-ti-ful feel-in',
> Ev-'ry-thin's go-in' my way.[8]

Following is the division of syllables that will give the vowels their greatest sustaining value.

> Oh, wha-ta beau-ti-ful mo-rnin',
> Oh, wha-ta beau-ti-ful day,
> I go-ta beau-ti-ful fee-lin',
> E-v'ry-thi-n'sgo-in' my way.

Note that the lengthening of vowels is accomplished by tacking the ending consonants on to the beginning of the next syllable or word. Even though this procedure makes the division of syllables look strange in print, the effect in singing is quite natural.

In order to be consistent with the role of Curly, who is an uneducated cowhand, the *t*'s in *what, beautiful,* and *got* need to be softened, sounding almost like *d*'s. The *i* in *beautiful* should not sound like *ee,* but rather like the *i* in *tin.* The *r* in *mornin'* should be the American *r,* the tip of the tongue slightly raised. Care must be taken, however, that the *r* be unexaggerated, since this would interfere with the open vowel *o* which precedes it. The exaggerated, midwestern *r* is appropriate only in comedy or character material.

The original lyric of "Younger Than Springtime" *(South Pacific)*, as it appears in the printed vocal score is:

> Young-er than Spring-time are you,
> Soft-er than star-light are you.[9]

The rules of standard English state that the letter *r* is not pronounced before a consonant or pause. The elimination of the *r* makes for a smoother connection of vowels, and consequently enables the singer to produce a more legato melodic line. Thus:

> You-nga than Spri-ngtime ah-you,
> So-fta than stah-light ah-you,

Care must be exercised in eliminating the *r* so that the result is not a phony British accent. The final sound in *younger* and *softer* should not be *a* as in *father*, but as in *sofa* (the so-called neutral vowel).

The alternate version, a more colloquial one, allows the pronunciation of the letter *r*. This version results in a more American (pop) sound.

> You-nger than Spri-ngtime a-ryou,
> So-fter than sta-rlight a-ryou.

Both versions are acceptable, and the choice of one over the other should be dictated by the character's speech in the play.

The original printed version of "If I Loved You" *(Carousel)* is:

> If I loved you,
> Time and again I would try to say
> All I'd want you to know.[10]

The division of syllables for singing:

> I-fI lo-vedyou,
> Ti-meandagai-nIwouldtry to say
> A-lII-'dwantyou to know.

The lyrical quality of the song and its soaring vocal line require the utmost legato singing—the tying together of the notes.

In the first line care must be taken that *loved* does not sound like *love*—a common error. Likewise, the *d* in *I'd want you to know* must be clearly articulated.

The diphthong in *time* requires the broad *a* to be held for the full value of the note, and the *i* sound blended into the next word, resulting in something that looks like ta-a-aim.

In general, diphthongs (sounds made up of two vowels on the same syllable) are governed by strict rules in legitimate singing. The first vowel (always the more open one) is given the full value of the note, and the second is quickly tossed off. The reason for this is to allow for greater vocal sonority and also to keep the throat as open as possible. "Pieces of Dreams" (Bergman and Legrand) is a good example of a song abounding in diphthongs such as *boy, found, round, find,* and *mind.*

Although the above described manner of singing diphthongs will produce the most legato vocal line, the popular singer need not be pedantic in applying the rules. As always, the expressive needs of the words and the feelings behind them should dictate the manner of pronunciation.

Time should be allowed to experiment with these sounds. For instance, a gradual rather than abrupt transition from the first to the second vowel is especially suited to certain phrases that call for intimacy. A study of how the best artists in both legitimate and popular singing vary the pronunciation of diphthongs can be rewarding.

The original version (the last ten bars) of "A Foggy Day" from the film *Damsel in Distress* is:

> For, sud-den-ly, I saw you there
> And through fog-gy London town the sun was shi-ning
> ev-'ry-where.[11]

The division of syllables for singing:

> For, su-dden-ly, I saw you there
> An-dthrough fo-ggy Lon-ndon town the sun-nwas shi-ning
> e-v'ry-where.

As before, the manner of pronouncing the *r*'s is optional.

The *d* of *an-dthrough* almost disappears. However, if *and* is to be stressed, *and through* should be separated.

The *n*'s of *London* and *sun* may be sustained, as can the *ng* of *shining*. Although in legitimate singing the sustaining of the nasal sounds *m, n,* and *ng* is carefully avoided, in musical theater and popular singing these sounds are frequently used as additional colors in the vocal palette. There are many examples of the stunning use of this effect by such artists as Frank Sinatra, Judy Garland (in her recording of this very song), Barbra Streisand, and many others.

There are times when diction adjustments must be made, not for reasons of style or esthetics, but for the sheer practicality of facilitating musical execution. For instance, if a song ends on a high note on the vowel *ee* or *oo,* it may be difficult to sing, especially if it is to be sung loudly. Due to the small mouth conformation that these two vowels require, the volume of sound is reduced. The solution to the problem is to "cheat" on the vowel. For instance, if the last word of the song is *you* and it is to be sung on a high note, the vowel is altered from *oo* to *uh*. This is the case with the final line of "Everything's Coming Up Roses" *(Gypsy)*. The last line ends on a climactic high note on the word *you*. By changing the final *you* to *yuh,* the mouth can be opened somewhat more and a bigger sound can then be projected. Similarly, if the vowel is *ee,* it can be changed to *eh,* as in met.

Since a constant comparison has been made between legitimate singing (art songs, opera, oratorio) on one hand and musical theater and popular singing on the other, let us put the two side by side and note the differences relevant to diction.

Legitimate Music	*Musical Theater* or *Popular Music*
Vowel sounds are standardized; minimal adjustments are made to fit the role or the character of the music.	Vowel sounds are adjusted to fit the role or the character of the music.

Legitimate Music	*Musical Theater* or *Popular Music*
Diphthongs are uniformly pronounced. The first vowel is given the maximum duration, the second is quickly appended.	Diphthongs may be pronounced as they are in legitimate music, or they may be altered for expressive reasons.
The letter *r* is always omitted before a consonant or pause. When it *is* pronounced, it is always in the English manner, the tip of the tongue flipping against the upper gum ridge.	The letter *r* *may* be omitted before a consonant or a pause. When it *is* pronounced, it is always in the American manner.
With the exception of folklike material, the language of legitimate music is that of educated English.	The language used in musical theater depends on the nature of the character, his education, and the region of his origin. The language of popular music derives from contemporary colloquial usage.

Musical theater favors diction that enhances believability and naturalness. Congruence is sought between the sung and spoken word.

Popular music allows the greatest freedom of pronunciation and there are very few rules. Whatever criteria might be said to prevail derive from the influence of the particular recording artists who find public acceptance. The quality of diction in recordings ranges from wonderful to execrable, from exquisite clarity to raucous incomprehensibility.

ENERGY AND CLIMAX

One of the common faults of inexperienced performers is giving too much too soon. The performer will begin a song with all the stops pulled out—the body in motion, eyes flashing, the voice at maximum volume, the hard sell. Naturally, starting at such an extreme level of energy, there is no place to go, and the best the performer can hope for is to be able to maintain the frantic outpouring until the end, an exhausting and self-defeating endeavor. A sense of desperation often lurks behind such mindless squandering of energy, as if the performer were afraid to ease up for fear of revealing his insecurities. Energy *per se* has no value. It becomes meaningful only if it is used to carry out a design or a specific task.

A song, poem, or play is most often designed so that it accumulates interest and excitement from beginning to end. Somewhere near the end is a high point or climax, which can be compared to the discharge of accumulated energy. The charging up is not in the form of a smooth, continuous arc, but a jagged upward line, consisting of a series of uneven jumps. Each jump corresponds to the unfolding of new information in the lyric or the introduction of an unusual rhythm in the melody. The repetition of phrases contributes to the charging up process. Vivid imagery, striking harmonic changes, and the use of suspense all work together to build toward a climax. The climax itself comes at that part of the lyric where the story unravells emotionally and reveals itself. The musical climax, which is usually the highest pitch near the end of the song, most often coincides with the lyrical climax. For instance, in "As Long As He Needs Me," both musical and lyrical climaxes fall on the very last line of the song. In "A Foggy Day," on the other hand, the lyrical climax comes on

> *But suddenly, I saw you there—*
> And through foggy London Town
> The sun was shining ev'rywhere.

Musically, however, the high point comes on the word *shining.*

In such cases, it is the performer's choice to stress one or the other climax. There is greater strength in choosing one, rather than dividing the energy between two climaxes. (The author's choice in this example would be to stress the lyrical climax.)

In considering the performer's energy separately from the energy inherent in the words and music, two aspects must be distinguished from each other. First, we speak of inner energy, which can be variously called intensity, concentration, or involvement. This must be in continuous operation, since any diminution is instantly perceived by the audience and interpreted as lack of communication. The other kind of performing energy is external, and it expresses itself in movement, dance, gesture, facial expression, and voice. Here the performer has many options. Whether for artistic or practical reasons, he may move and gesture or be still, use his full voice or conserve it. For instance, the careful pacing of the voice is an important factor in any performance. Every singer has limits beyond which he cannot push his voice without damage. For example, he may be able to safely sing a two-bar phrase fortissimo, but not the entire chorus of a song. He must therefore map out the song during practice sessions and determine where he can conserve his voice so that he has enough strength for the long, demanding phrases in high tessitura. Difficult songs like "The Miller's Son" *(A Little Night Music)* and "Another Hundred People" *(Company)* certainly require such planning. Aside from endurance, there must be an apportioning of physical and vocal effort so that a sense of increasing excitement and a continuously forward movement is achieved.

As for stage movement and gesture (which will be discussed in Chapter 10), it is difficult to generalize how much is appropriate. It is impressive how little a superior performer seems to be doing. He may be motionless for long periods of time, his face and eyes may not show much expression, or his voice may seem rather ordinary. Yet he holds the attention of the audience which waits with keen excitement for his next word or note. What is the answer? How does he do so much with so little effort? The answer is that he does it with *seemingly* little effort. There is much going on under the surface that may pass unnoticed. The inner concentration is fully turned on, the images are alive in the mind, and the feelings are in tune with the text and the melody. However, the performer chooses to understate for the moment and to hold back the physical expression of his thoughts and feelings. This technique may be completely intuitive, or it may be learned. Most likely, it is a combination of intuition and experience that has taught him how powerful a tool understatement can be.

Such delaying tactics in holding back excitement richly pay off when the moment finally arrives when he lets go. This final peak of intensity would not be possible without the preceding underplaying; the one is directly related to the other. (Note that "letting go" does not imply singing loudly or indulging in much movement. It simply means going beyond a self-imposed barrier.)

Exercise

Sing a ballad that is familiar to you and be aware of energy as it ebbs and flows. Notice where your imagination is stimulated, where your feelings become involved, and where the narrative seems to peak.

Now sing it again. This time be aware of energy in purely musical terms. Note the effect of rhythmic figures, the rise and fall of melodic shapes, and take special note of the places where both words and music surge simultaneously.

Do the lyrical and melodic climaxes coincide? If not, choose one and give it your maximum effort.

After performing the piece several times in this way, perform it again freely, with no thought of analysis. Sing it purely from the standpoint of feeling and intuition. Notice any changes that have taken place.

Exercise

Now practice understatement. Take a ballad such as "My Funny Valentine" or "The Party's Over" and experiment with energy distribution. With your inner concentration fully turned on, restrain all outward signs of it until a chosen moment. See how long you can delay the outward excitement leading to the climax. Try different ways of expressing the climax—loudly, softly—and find the way that feels right for you.

ENDINGS

The way that the last notes of a song are sung deserves special attention. Aside from artistic considerations, the end of the song is followed by the audience response, signaling approval or disapproval.

Of course, throughout the performance the audience has, in a manner of speaking, been "talking" back to the performer. Through attentive silence or fidgety rustling, through tears or laughter, excitement or yawns, it has shown its interest or boredom. The performer has been carefully listening to these messages during the course of the song and used them as corrective feedback.

The end of the song is the culmination of all that has preceded it. It is the moment of the song's highest energy, regardless of whether it ends in a high or low register. It is the gathering together of the story line, the melodic structure, and all the feeling elements that bring to the audience a sense of finality and, hopefully, satisfaction.

However, the convergence of these powerful forces does not automatically assure a successful outcome. The performer has the power to augment or diminish the final effect depending on whether she can really achieve a satisfactory finish.

Following are some points worth considering:

- The audience should know well in advance that the end of the song is approaching. To be caught off guard by an abrupt or unexpected ending is a disconcerting experience for the listener and is bound to lessen the appreciation of the performance. On the other hand, a well-prepared finish gives the listener time to respond in an appropriate manner.

- In a ballad, the broadcasting of the ending is usually accomplished by a slowing down (retarding) of tempo.

- In a fast tune, a continuous build-up of vocal energy at the end is needed, together with some kind of melodic extension or repetition of the last phrase of music. (See Appendix A for further ideas on this subject.)

- Whether your last note is held until the very end of the song or the orchestra (or pianist) has a short postlude after your last note, *do not break your concentration* for at least several seconds after you have finished. (The length depends on the mood that has been created; atmospheric pieces require more time than joyful, rhythmic pieces.) If the mood of the song is introspective, take time before re-establishing eye contact with the audience.

- Concentration, of course, extends to your physical bearing. There should be no collapsing of posture or allowing the eyes to aimlessly wander through the audience as if to ask "did you like me?"

- Walking off stage after your last number is also a part of your performance. You are still visible to your audience, and your communication with it should continue until you are out of sight.

THE BODY
AND MOVEMENT

III

The Body
and Movement

9

In the sense that any activity is a form of motion, and since a multitude of activities occur in the body simultaneously, the body can be said to be in continuous motion. Some of these activities are internal and are unconsciously controlled as, for instance, the movement of brain waves, the peristaltic movements of the alimentary system, blood circulation, and the secretions of the body. Then there are semiautonomous systems like breathing and heart beat that can be partially controlled. These activities (movements) of the body serve to maintain and regulate the vital processes.

Another class of activities are those that are consciously directed by the brain and that allow us the use of our limbs and other parts of the body in myriad ways. This type of movement makes possible the differentiation of individual muscles and the learning of complicated skills such as dancing and sports.

There is yet another kind of movement that has special importance to the performer, since it spontaneously reflects the state of mind and is thus

103

highly communicative. We will call these sympathetic movements. They are neither autonomously controlled, nor consciously willed. They are by nature responsive, reacting to mental images. William James, the great American psychologist, was among the first to notice this phenomenon and to assert that every thought or mental image contains the seeds of an action, that it is the natural impulse of human beings to externalize their mental life. The body actually *does* reflect and register mental states in various ways. At times these sympathetic responses are felt as internal bodily signals: twinges, pains, or pleasurable feelings. Or they may express themselves more visibly through eye movements, facial expressions, or the contraction and/or relaxation of a muscle or groups of muscles.

The range of these responses is broad. They may be so subtle as to be imperceptible to all but the most discerning eye or grossly obvious.

Let us demonstrate with a simple experiment.

> Sit in a comfortable chair, close your eyes, and relax. Let your arms lie inert in your lap. Now visualize yourself lifting a heavy weight with your right arm. Hold it for ten seconds, focusing your attention on the lifting arm. If your visualization has been vivid and concentrated, you should feel a very slight but perceptible contracton in the lifting muscles of your right arm. Next, your eyes still closed, imagine a vehicle moving from left to right. You will probably become aware that your eye muscles are contracting as if you actually saw the vehicle moving.[1]

These sympathetic movements, though minute, can be augmented appreciably if the visualization is coupled with emotional content. Imagining someone falling off a high building may cause you to feel a slight clutch in your stomach. If the imagined person is someone dear to you, the sensation would be greatly intensified, and a spasm might be experienced in the body. By contrast, the visualization of you and your loved one lying in front of a warm fireplace probably will induce a sensation of warmth, accompanied by the loosening of muscles and a feeling of relaxation.

Note the interrelatedness of imagery, sensation, emotion, and movement. We can see now why imagery is such a potent expressive tool. *Imagery literally moves us.* The significance of this for the actor is

[1]Samuel W. Gutwirth, *You Can Learn To Relax*, p.13-17.

enormous, since it is the basis for spontaneous movement. If the actor is sensitive to imagery, he need only somewhat exaggerate these tiny impulses and they will emerge as full movements.

Spontaneous movements also occur as responses to actions. If someone lifts a hand to strike you, your body contracts in anticipation, and you take a step backward to avoid the blow. Sometime later you remember the incident and relive it. You re-experience the contraction in your body and the backward movement, but on a much reduced scale. It has become a mini-version of the original reaction.

The psychological counterpart to being physically threatened or actually struck is to have a thought or feeling that corresponds to the physical act. For instance, someone makes a cutting remark to you. As with the physical act, you flinch inwardly (a movement). You may now choose to suppress the expression of that movement ("I won't give you the satisfaction of knowing that you have hurt me"), or you may allow it to register and show surprised indignation, coupled, perhaps, with a slight backward movement. The two reactions are identical, except that the first case has been censored, and the second case has been allowed expression.

Thus, spontaneous movement can occur in response to thoughts, feelings, images, and actions. The way we react to these stimuli depends on our personalities and what we consider socially appropriate.

The individual whose feelings are unblocked and who is unburdened with social, moral, or religious taboos can react to a situation with some choice, as in the above example. On the other hand, the individual who is frozen in his responses by such social constraints will be perceived as dull, unfeeling, and unresponsive.

THE LOSS OF SPONTANEITY

If we retrace our steps and try to assign causes for our loss of spontaneity, how we started from a state of naturalness and freedom of movement and became imitators and mimics of others, we may find the following:

- There is a loss of self-confidence. Somewhere along the way we have picked up the notion that the real self is not good enough to be shown in its natural state, and that it must be replaced with something better.

- We imitate bad models. Parents and parent surrogates, the people who are most influential in our early lives, have lost *their* spontaneity and naturalness. If they are stiff and up-tight, it's understandable that the child takes this to be the norm.

- We lose grace and efficiency of movement because we are *taught* to be ashamed of our bodies. Excessive criticism of the child's body, of weight gain, or of real or imagined blemishes can cause a rejection of one's own body.

- To function efficiently, society demands of the individual a great number of behavior controls. However, when these controls become too restrictive, the individual may suffer serious loss of functioning. If the particular environment frowns on the overt expression of feelings, the individual becomes accustomed to holding back anger, masking fear or withholding affection. These inhibitions of natural feelings are then associated with muscular contractions which, in time become frozen into chronic conditions of tightness and awkwardness.[2]

- Anxiety, which is a learned condition, is a powerful deterrent to free movement. When we are anxious, we experience involuntary muscular contractions. These contractions often oppose other muscle groups that are trying to perform some task, causing a locking or freezing sensation which performers sometimes experience. Futhermore, anxiety is always accompanied by reduced breathing, which deprives the body of sufficient oxygen, resulting in desensitization or numbing of the body.

- We lose the spontaneous and efficient use of our bodies through nonuse. A body that is not properly exercised and conditioned cannot be an expressive instrument in the service of a demanding art.

Spontaneity is a relative term: To become completely spontaneous is neither possible nor desirable. Deliberation and control are the balancing qualities that every individual needs in order to be a functioning member of any group. Nonetheless, it seems that most individuals, including performers, are overbalanced in the direction of control and would benefit by being able to allow their intuitive natures to express themselves more readily. Because an unpremeditated action shows a willingness on the part of the performer to take a risk, it is also exciting to an audience.

However, counteracting the influences that interfere with spontaneity is a formidable task, since conditioning starts at birth. One of the difficulties is, that we must grow in awareness in our thinking, sensing, feeling, and acting in order to do so. Growing awareness may be accompa-

---

[2]For a detailed account of the process of body armoring, read *Bioenergetics* by Alexander Lowen.

nied by discomfort. For example, if we have learned to cover up our lack of self-confidence by assuming an aggressive attitude, our awareness of this fact will make us self-conscious. However, as the realization grows that the defensive attitude is not necessary and that the real person beneath the facade is valid and worthy, spontaneous actions may begin.

If we have imitated bad models to the point that they have become a part of us, awareness may lead to a rejection of the imitation, but it will also cause us to feel naked and unsupported until we feel more confident of our genuine resources.

For instance, it is common for a performer who finds it difficult to express tenderness and vulnerbility to compensate by limiting herself to a repertoire of big, vocally impressive songs. If she were, through awareness, to reject such material and perform songs that require tenderness, discomfort and frustration are sure to be experienced during the transition period. Change requires both overcoming the resistance to change and the willingness to suffer the inevitable, but temporary anxiety and distress that are the consequences of change.

An important part of the relearning process is the recognition of the symptoms of anxiety, the shortness of breath, the muscular contractions of the jaw, tongue, or throat and learning to endure these as we try to reorient our attitudes. (See Appendix C for further discussion on anxiety.)

STEREOTYPES

Most people do not want to be viewed as part of a category but as individuals. The idea that a person lacks qualities that distinguish her from others is offensive to most people. Americans so pride themselves on their individuality that they often refer to it as a national trait.

There are, however, also strong traditional forces in society that contradict this view and tend to pull the individual in the direction of conformity and facelessness. Mass population, mass production, computerization, and other depersonalizers all encourage anonymity.

These contrary pulls exert their influence on a child from the earliest years. Depending on personal propensities and circumstances, a bias in one or the other direction develops. Unfortunately, the general trend is in the direction of conformity, and the signs of it are everywhere.

While conformity in everyday life may or may not be condoned, the abandonment of individuality in the arts is unthinkable, since a performer's uniqueness is her greatest gift to an audience.

The preciousness of that gift is often not appreciated by young and inexperienced performers, and they are particularly susceptible to the influence of trends, fads and the stars and superstars of the entertainment world. By the time young people leave high school, many influences have shaped their performing styles, and they come to performing schools fully equipped with vocal styles, postural mannerisms, and assorted bags of "schtick." The irony, of course, is that the singers, dancers, and actors they imitate *are* individuals. By the act of imitation, these young students only negate themselves.

To be truly individual requires self-confidence and a willingness to take risks and the consequences of those risks. These qualities usually come with time and experience, after many failures have taught the performer where her strengths lie.

AWARENESS OF STEREOTYPES

Who were your singing idols when you were going to high school? What qualities attracted you to these performers? Are you aware of their influence on you now? Do you think that they have helped you become a better performer? In what way?

Here are suggested ways of becoming more conscious of your mannerisms:

- Ask a few performer friends whose opinions you respect to give you some honest feedback.
- Make some tapes of yourself and listen to your voice carefully with respect to vocal idiosyncrasies.
- Have someone film you as you perform.

Examining yourself in these different ways should give you a fresh perspective. Try to objectively evaluate yourself as if you were someone else. Which qualities seem genuine and which false?

You may find that some of the borrowed mannerisms are purely physical imitations as, for instance, Judy Garland passing her fingers through her hair while singing. On the other hand, you may have been inspired by Garland's wonderful concentration of feeling and her ability to involve herself completely in a song. The first influence should obviously be abandoned, while the second could have a very positive effect on your development as a performer.

Exercise

Make a list of all the undesirable mannerisms that you want to eliminate. Cultivate your awareness of them. Experiment with the following ways of performing:

1. *Do nothing.* Rather than using your hands and arms in your usual stereo-typed way, just stand there and sing, doing nothing else with your body. You may find that eliminating all movement in this manner creates tension. This is understandable, since you will feel exposed and vulnerable. Therefore, try to relax your body before you start and watch for tension creeping in.

2. *Do the contrary.* If your habitual way of singing a ballad is to move with slow, graceful gestures, do the opposite and make discontinuous, more rapid movements. If you always plant yourself firmly on the ground, change your weight from one foot to the other occasionally or walk around as you sing.

3. *Act out a song absolutely literally.* Literalness of movement is commonly considered to be the mark of the amateur. However, our intention is to break away from set patterns of performing and find alternative ways. You may find out that although acting out a lyric can be terribly clichéd, at times it can also be very appropriate.

4. *Dance the lyric.* Have your pianist play the song and improvise a dance to it. You can do this in several ways. First, let your movements suggest the general mood and atmosphere of the song without trying to coordinate them with the tempo. Second, pantomime the song. Act it out as if for a deaf audience. Do not mouth the words in either versions.

Obviously, these exercises are intended to be used as practice explorations. However, it often happens that a movement or gesture will emerge that can be incorporated into the final performance.

COORDINATION OF SINGING AND MOVEMENT

When singing and movement are combined, synchronization occurs. If the performer is walking while singing, the walk will be in time with the music; gestures and facial comments will fall on the strong beats of the music; even the blinking of the eyes will be coordinated with the tempo.

Such synchrony is a natural response and is evidence of our instinctual need to integrate the various elements of behavior. We see this coordination in the movements of children when they sing, in the folk songs of all nations, and in popular forms of music such as jazz, rock, gospel.

For the purpose of dramatic realism, it is occasionally necessary to break up this synchrony of voice and movement so that each can be presented independently. If a song is to be performed in a naturalistic manner without any break in acting styles from the scene that precedes it, it may be fitting to use body movement independent of the music. There can still be partial synchrony for the purpose of accenting a particular word here or there, but the persistent reinforcement of rhythm by means of physical expression would in this case be eliminated. To be able to do this, the performer must have sufficient control of body coordination so that he has the choice of moving in synchrony or independently. The choice should be based on the nature of the music on one hand and the dramatic necessities on the other. Generally, strongly rhythmic music will require correspondingly rhythmic body participation, and calm, slow music can be treated more freely.

Moving independently of the musical pulse does not come naturally to most performers. Hence, the following exercise.

Independence
of Singing and Movement

1. *Walking while singing.* Sing a moderately paced song like "People Will Say We're in Love" (*Oklahoma*). Have a pianist accompany you, keeping a steady tempo. As you sing, walk around the room *out of tempo* with the music. This may feel awkward, since the tendency to integrate music and movement is strong. Nevertheless, persist until you can achieve independence without sacrificing musical or lyrical values. Try this exercise with songs that have different tempos and rhythmic character. Note the effect of these elements on your coordination.

2. *Random movements while singing.* While singing a song in a steady tempo, perform various random actions. For example, pick up a book and open it; sit in a chair, then get up; pick up an object (real or imaginary) from the floor; untie, then tie your shoe laces. Take time in performing these actions. Don't try to crowd too many into a short interval. Continue for several choruses. Notice whether you act on the strong or weak beats of the music.

3. *Random attention to your person.* While singing, attend to yourself in some

way. Pass your hand through your hair: look at your ring or bracelet, then turn it slightly; straighten your skirt or jacket. As before, don't rush.

Although the actions performed in these exercises are random and irrelevant, they should be executed purposefully.

TRANSFORMING IMAGES TO MOVEMENT

Throughout this book it has been stressed that the singing actor's most potent resources are his imagination and his personal life history, that between these two elements the total range of human experiences can be portrayed, provided that the imagination is active and fertile and the life experiences open to recall.

Another point that has been made repeatedly is that of the interrelatedness of physical, emotional, and mental activities and how these are constantly transformed into some kind of movement, be it covert or visible. One such transformation was described in Chapter 6, on the physicalization of emotion. In that process, starting with an intellectual interpretation of the words and giving that interpretation a physical expression, an emotional response (movement) was elicited.

In the method that follows, these components are rearranged to encourage spontaneous movement through imagery. Since our physiology already has a built-in reaction to mental images, we will use these minute signals. By exaggerating the body's reactions to the images, sensations are heightened. By further stepping up these sensations, movement results.

The following exercises will clarify the process.

Exercise

Choose a descriptive word that relates to one of the five senses such as hot, fragrant, bitter, howling, or green. Now associate each of these adjectives with a noun. For example:

hot stove
fragrant flower
sour apple
howling wind
green meadow

Next, with eyes closed, choose one image and dwell on it. Notice whether you feel any physical sensation in connection with it. If you think of *hot stove,* perhaps you imagine touching a hot stove and being burned. You may become aware of a tiny inward flinching resulting from this image. Exaggerate the flinching somewhat. What muscles in your body become contracted? Now, without exaggeration, go back to your first reaction to the image. Do you still feel the same muscles contracting ever so slightly? Try this experiment again with eyes open.

Choosing another context for the words, you may imagine warming yourself by a hot stove on a cold winter night. The physical reaction to this image will, of course, be quite different now. You may feel an expansive radiation loosening the muscles of your body, a feeling of thawing out. Again, exaggerate these sensations until they become visible; then return to the original response.

Whenever possible, use each pair of words in contrasting ways, as in the above example. Spend several minutes with each image. Take another example, *sour apple.* First, simply visualize a green apple and let some association come of itself. Possibly a person who is a sour apple may come to mind. Be sensitive to your body and on the lookout for signs of responses. Depending on whether you feel distaste, anger, or contempt for this person, tiny reflections of the attitude will register somewhere in you. Exaggerate, then come back to the original response.

In contrast, if you imagine biting into a sour apple, you may feel your mouth pucker, saliva flow, and slight contractions occur in parts of the body.

Exercise

Next is a series of phrases related to motion:

> running up the stairs
> reaching for a fruit high in a tree
> pushing against an adversary
> pulling a rope
> throwing a football
> falling off a fence
> swimming against a strong current
> jumping off a diving board
> (Add to the list.)

Using the same procedure as before, vividly imagine the action taking place in your mind and be sensitive to body responses. For instance, in the image of running up the stairs, what do you notice happening to your leg or stomach muscles? Has your breathing increased somewhat? As before, exaggerate whatever sensation comes to your awareness. Thus, if you notice your breathing becoming deeper, breathe even more deeply. If you feel a slight contraction in your stomach muscles, contract them even more. Note that the resultant physical sensations fall into several broad categories:

> the contracting of muscles
> the relaxation of muscles
> feelings of attraction
> feelings of repulsion

Note that the attraction-repulsion effect is both mental and physical.

Images of a loved one instinctively make us lean forward and reach out. Similarly, images relating to fear, disdain, or contempt cause the body to lean away in a reaction of avoidance. Whether or not the performer reacts to his inner messages (assuming that he is aware of them) depends on interpretive factors and questions of style. Certainly, these reactions are not intended to be used in the manner of a formula—that would be creating another stereotype. Rather, the intention is to develop a consciousness of the power of images to move us (literally), as well as a sensitivity to what goes on in our bodies. If we can then let these forces express themselves in the most natural and authentic way, we are being spontaneous.

Let us take a specific example and apply this idea.

The mood of "Over the Rainbow" (see lyrics on page 84) is one of yearning for a better place—a hopefulness about things to come. This is coupled with a feeling of sadness and the knowledge that this wished-for better world is, after all, only a dream. The images are rich in sensory content, and there is much potential for spontaneous movement inherent in them. Observe the particular sense that is involved in each image and how the body responds.

For instance, every stanza begins with a description of open spaces and great distances. The feeling is one of being strongly drawn to a beautiful vision. The effect of this on the body is that of loosening the muscles and allowing expansion. Lines 3 and 4 introduce an aural sensation (lullaby), again coupled with distance and time. Opposing the feeling of openness and relaxation is the yearning to be *over the rainbow*. This represents tension and muscular contraction, a reaching for something that is beyond reach. (How does the body express two contrary feelings?)

In lines 9 and 10, troubles (*clouds*) are avoided through magical solutions (*wish upon a star* and *melt like lemon drops*). This image contains elements of repulsion and turning away.

Lines 13 and 14 again evoke a feeling of distance and visual imagery (being drawn upward, attracted).

Without warning, line 18, *why then, oh why, can't I?*, dashes the singer down to earth and back to reality (an image of falling from a height?). It has all been a wishful dream. The hopes are deflated (muscles deflated). The pull of reality is stronger than the dream. Yet on the repetition of *why, oh why, can't I?* (line 20), the melody soars upward to a new peak, while the words remain below—a perfect musical representation of the contrary pulls of the wished-for and the real.

LISTENING, RESPONDING, AND MOVING

The following exercise should be practiced to music that has occasional changes of mood or tempo. Program music, such as tone poems, descriptive music, and film scores can be used.[3] If the music is unfamiliar, so much the better.

Exercise

In a quiet place where there will be no distractions, play a recording of such music. For a while simply listen, allowing the music to enter you and affect you as it will. After a time, gradually start to bring your body into movement by simply responding to the music. Do not try to "perform" or achieve anything; only follow the music with your attention and let your thoughts and feelings go where the music leads you. Close your eyes and

---

[3]See Helen L. Bonny and Louis M. Savary, *Music and Your Mind* (New York: Harper & Row, 1973) for an excellent list of recordings that are suitable for this exercise.

notice whether this facilitates your journey. Allow yourself to associate; let memories and fantasies emerge and mingle freely. Be aware of the way the music makes contact with you. Does it make your insides move? Do the colors and moods of the music calm or excite you? Do they arouse images, feelings, or kinesthetic sensations?

1. *Variant I:* Now make your movements coincide with the rhythms and tempo of the music. Observe the strong beats and let your body duplicate them. When the music rises to excitement and tension, let your body mirror these sensations. Be alternately extravagant and subtle in your movements.

2. *Variant II:* Have your pianist play a song that you are learning. Have him play it freely so that you can't anticipate his tempos or phrasing. Without singing, allow yourself to respond to his playing in the manner of the first exercise. Simply move as the music suggests itself to you.

After doing this a while, very gradually bring your voice in. At first you may only speak a word here or there, then sing a phrase, then be silent for an interval. Gradually sing more and more, all the while moving with the song, until you are singing the entire song. As before, let all this happen quite easily and spontaneously. Let your attitude be one of curiosity and exploration.

After you have finished, be silent and replay in your mind what you have just done. Recall your body sensations and movements. Were you surprised at some of the movements that resulted? Can you duplicate them? Could you incorporate them into an actual performance?

MOVEMENT AND THE RHYTHMIC SENSE

We have all heard singers who seem to have an adequate sense of rhythm, keep good time, observe note values correctly, and so forth, but who nevertheless are dull and unexciting. We may say that they don't have a "feel" for rhythm. However, this evaluation does not specify what the problems are.

Closer examination often reveals that in such cases there is an absence of body involvement; the head and voice perform alone. The separation of head and body creates an effect of awkwardness and unreality, as if the voice were coming out of a mannequin. When there *is* body movement, it is added in a manner that is unrelated to the content and feeling values of the song, or in some cases may actually contradict what the song is trying to say.

On the other hand, when we observe singers who *do* have a rhythmic feel, we observe the following:

- The performer exhibits much personal involvement and excitement.
- The accentuation of words is in synchrony with the corresponding accents of the music. This, however, is not done in a predictable manner, and variety is achieved through contrast, elongation or shortening of words (notes) in order to avoid rhythmic monotony. Further, the accentuation is visible in terms of body movement, gesture, and facial expressions.
- There is good rapport between the singer and the accompaniment that supports him. The singer is able to be in and out of synchrony because he is constantly aware of the fundamental pulse of the music. Such control of rhythmic expression is best illustrated by singer-guitarists or singer-pianists, who while playing their own accompaniment in a steady tempo, can nevertheless phrase freely against it. Such independence extends also to body movement.
- The performer's movements seem graceful and easy; they seem to be generated by the music.

The latter observation is another example of the integration that constantly takes place in the body: one element (musical rhythm) activating another (physical movement). This corresponds closely to the relationship between imagery and movement that was discussed earlier. Both imagery and rhythm seem to act as catalysts in this respect.

The power of music to influence behavior has only recently been researched, and out of these studies the field of music therapy is emerging. For example, it is now common knowledge that if one listens to a piece of music with a tempo that is the same as one's heartbeat, and that tempo is increased or decreased, the heartbeat will similarly increase or decrease. Psychological states can also be strongly influenced by the kind of music one listens to. Shelley Winters describes the film director George Stevens having a set of push buttons at the edge of his director's chair.[4] Knowing which kind of music would activate a particular feeling in an actor, he

---

[4]Lewis Funke and John E. Booth, *Actors Talk About Acting,* Part I, p. 157.

would cause the appropriate music to be played while a scene was being filmed. (In those days, the dialogue was dubbed in at a later stage of the film making; thus, hearing the music during the "take" caused no problems.)

Such reactions to music are, of course, subliminal and out of reach of consciousness. The individual responds to the music, but on an automatic level. However, if we can bring that sensitivity to awareness, the individual can gain control over it. (In our next experiment we will try to heighten awareness by isolating one element of music, rhythm, from the rest.)

CHANTING

Chanting, the singing on a monotone or a very narrow range of pitch, is an effective device for activating the rhythmic sense. This very basic and primitive form of vocal expression has been used for countless ages for a variety of purposes. When used in groups, chanting acts as a powerful reinforcer of feelings, as in mass rallies and sporting events. It facilitates group work where synchronous efforts are required, as in work gangs. There are chants sung in conjunction with dancing that are used in celebrations and rituals. And children, of course, love to chant and improvise them easily.

The major characteristic of chants is the repetitive use of words and the satisfaction and pleasure this invariably arouses. Of course, there are also religious chants that are used for very different reasons.

It seems that vocal repetition is energizing, and that at a certain point the repetition impels the body to participate. This effect is seen in individual chanting as well as mass chanting, although inevitably there is some diminution of excitement due to the loss of group reinforcement.

The exercise that follows is most effectively used in rhythmic pieces. By reducing the melody to a chant and setting up a repetitive pattern of words (drawn from some part of the song, usually the first few measures), a build-up of energy occurs during which the physical involvement of the body inevitably follows.

Exercise

Choose a moderate or fast tempo song that has a strong rhythmic pulse, e.g., "Another Hundred People," "I Got Rhythm," or "Applause, Applause!"

Take the first or the last line and chant it on a monotone. Keep repeating it ad infinitum. Use no accompaniment. Allow the excitement to generate through repetition alone. Thus:

Who could ask for anything more
" " " " " "
" " " " " "
" " " " " "

Keep your body loose and relaxed and allow it gradually to become integrated with the chant. After doing this for a while, you may find a number of reactions taking place: The body starts to sway with the rhythm. Certain words receive body emphasis.

After a further interval, allow yourself to alter the pitch of the notes in simple variations. Another variation may be tried: Fill the space at the end of each line with an exclamation of a sound.

Who could ask for anything more (uh!)
" " " " " " (yeah!)
" " " " " " (hey-*hey*)
" " " " " " (slap)

Other variations are as follows: Further truncate the line:

Anything more
Anything more
Anything more

Further yet:

More, more, more, more, more
More, more, more, more, more

(Try chanting this last variant in the rhythm of Glenn Miller's "A String of Pearls.")

Chanting, in the manner described above, should be viewed as a form of musical playfulness. Because it requires little skill, the tensions that often arise with the practice of the more demanding elements of performance are absent. The body loosens up and we are often able to perform dancelike movements that we thought ourselves incapable of.

There is another practical use to chanting that is related to musical arranging. The endings of musical numbers, especially those of up-tempo pieces, are almost invariably based on some form of repetitive musical pattern. It is this reinforcement of a rhythm through repetition that creates the excitement of a musical finish. It also allows the audience to prepare itself to respond to the performer at the end of the piece.

In the practice of chanting, one or several of the repetitive patterns will emerge that can be used as an ending section (coda) of an arrangement.

PUTTING IT TOGETHER

It is unfortunate that we cannot learn the art of performing in a holistic way, but have to learn the various skills that are necessary for performing in separate compartments, each taught by a specialist who is often out of touch with other specialists.

The complexity and sophistication of our way of life has had the effect of fragmentating the learning process. We learn things in small, seemingly unrelated parts, hoping to put them together again at some future time. We take separate lessons in singing technique, vocal interpretation, acting, ballet, modern, jazz, and tap dance. Then we wait for someone to tell us how to put it all together in a meaningful way. A stage director, a choreographer, or a musical director will show us how to integrate our skills so that they will fit into an overall concept of the musical play, television show, or nightclub presentation. To some extent, this is possible. The stage director can explain the central idea of the play, the atmospheric elements, the individual objectives of the actor, and other details. The choreographer can demonstrate how to make stage movement consistent with the style of the music, and the musical director can likewise give guidance regarding the needs of the musical score. However, in the limited time that is ordinarily available to stage a musical, whether on Broadway, summer stock, or television, the attention given the performer is most often inadequate to work out all the problems relating to his role. True, the general staging gets done—the obvious crossovers, the broad character strokes. But the fine points that will make the difference between hack work and artistry are often either neglected or left for the actor to work out alone. If there is any integrating to be done, it is the performer who must interrelate his skills so that all the fragments come together as a unified whole.

Thus, in his daily practice, no matter how detailed a particular problem may be, the connection to the whole performance must not be lost. The performer needs to develop a constant awareness of the strands that connect thought with action and voice with feeling. He must demand of himself utter consistency. No glorious high note, impressive moment, or arresting gesture should be done for its own sake, but only for the sake of a total performance and a unified concept. This concept must, in turn, derive from the essential statement that the lyric makes. Once this has been decided on, the preparation and working out of the song becomes a search for congruence with that statement so that all the details of musical nuance, dramatic utterance, and bodily inflections will flow together as one.

NIGHTCLUBS
IV

Nightclubs

10

Up to this point we have concerned ourselves with the singing actor performing in the context of musical forms that are centered around a story line or script—musical theater, opera, and television or film musicals. During the rehearsals for any of these works, a number of experts are on hand as part of the production staff to coach the performer in his respective skills: There are stage directors, musical directors, choreographers, costumers, make-up artists, and hair dressers. But more important to the performer than all these specialists is the script, since it is the blueprint upon which all his efforts are based. It tells him who he is, what happens to him, how he feels about people and a host of other details. Furthermore, it indicates in what manner or style he should express himself when he speaks, moves, or sings.

By contrast, when we enter the area of personal appearances in nightclubs and pop concerts, few of the above-mentioned conditions apply. There is no script upon which to base decisions regarding performance values and no staff of experts to coach and advise the performer. Along with arrangers, these can be hired, but they have to be sought out and paid, and the price for such services is usually very high. In this situation the singer is left to make almost all his own decisions in matters relating to his performance. He becomes, by necessity, his own producer and director, seeking out whatever help he can afford in the process of putting together his "act." Typically, if the singer is young and inexperienced, he will have to put together his material by himself, and his musical staff will consist of a single keyboard player or a guitarist.

However, there are also positive sides to the situation. For example, the performer now has immense freedom to express himself in any manner he wishes. With no script to impel him to perform in a particular way, he can choose a performance style that will show him to best advantage. For instance, he can have his musical accompaniment played in a new tempo and sing it in whatever key best suits him. He can give the song any interpretation he wants and create his own setting. He can decide to be himself or to portray some imaginary person; he can move or dance while he sings or stand still; he can address his audience directly or focus on some internal image. He is also free to choose his costumes, his make-up and his props; he may even have a say about the lighting and the sound system.

Even though such profusion of choices may sound attractive and desirable, many performers will on the contrary feel overwhelmed by the sheer number of possibilities, and the end product may turn out to be a haphazard mixture of ideas and styles or a falling back upon tired nightclub clichés.

A working scheme is needed that allows the performer freedom of choice, but gives him a framework upon which to base his performance and make coherent, meaningful decisions.

This brings us back to the concept of song as drama. Since the lyric of any song describes, to some degree, a human situation, it can be used as a basis for building a "script." It does not matter that some lyrics tell a complete story, and others are mere fragments or simply mood pieces. Every lyric has in it a seed idea which has the potential of being further developed and expanded; whatever is not explicit can become implicit by a creative use of the imagination.

Facing a volatile audience and performing under conditions that make concentration difficult, the nightclub performer can feel like a goldfish in a bowl. No wonder he often becomes self-conscious and resorts to wearing a mask to cover this vulnerability. When this happens, his attention is no longer on the song and its message but on himself, his external appearance, and the audience's approval.

In such a situation, having a script in mind can give the performer a comforting sense of security. The security comes in part from having to focus thoughts on very specific images. This helps keep him in contact with the song and encourages his involvement. By the very act of engaging his attention on these specifics, the script *dis*engages the performer from self-attention and negative self-evaluations.

THE SCRIPT

The central idea around the scripting of a song is to treat the song *as if* it evolved from an imagined situation or scene. This "scene," which is worked out during the preparation of the song, is the invention of the singer. Its contents may be based on real or imagined events. The only imperative is that it make sense with regard to the lyrics.

This process, incidentally, is quite similar to what happens when a musical show is put together—only in reverse. The creation of a musical usually begins with a book or play that is converted into a script, into which musical numbers are inserted at appropriate moments. In our process, we start with a song and then create a script to fit it.

The basic elements of the script are as follows:

1. *The words.* The lyrics of the song are the source of everything that follows. They provide the basis upon which the performer fills out the script through a series of imaginative choices.
2. *The setting.* Where does the action of the lyric take place?
3. *The character.* Who sings the song?
4. *The lead-in.* Why does the character sing (say) the words of the song?
5. *The audience.* How does the character relate to the audience?
6. *The musical arrangement.* In what musical idiom does the character express himself?

We will now need a model song to illustrate the step-by-step process that is about to follow. Although the scripting procedure can be applied to any kind of song, we will choose "As Long As He Needs Me" from *Oliver*.

This song, of course, already has a stage setting and dramatic context. In our version, however, we will reconceive the scene where the song occurs and give it a new context. This will give us the opportunity to exercise our imaginations and learn lessons by comparing our version with the original. In the course of rescripting the song we will also analyze it in detail, applying to it the various techniques that have been presented throughout the book.

Here are the lyrics to "As Long As He Needs Me":

As long as he needs me
Oh yes, he does need me.
In spite of what you see
I'm sure that *he* needs *me.*

(5)*Who else* would love him still
When they've been used *so* ill.
He knows I *always* will,
As long as he needs me.

(9)I miss him *so* much
When he is gone.
But when he's near me
I don't let on.

(13)The way I feel inside,
The love I have to hide,
The hell! I've got my pride
As long as he needs me.

(Interlude) (17) He doesn't say the things he should,
He acts the way he thinks he should,
But all the same, I'll play
The game *his* way.

(21) As long as he needs me
I *know* where I must be.
I'll cling on steadfastly
As long as he needs me.

(25) As long as life is long,
I'll love, him right or wrong.
And *somehow* I'll be *strong*
As long as he needs me.

(29)If you are lonely
Then you will know.
When someone needs you
You love them so.

(33)I won't betray his trust,
Though people say I must.
I've got to stay true, just
As long as he needs me.[1]

As a first step (assuming that the song is new to you), sing it through several times as well as you can to familiarize yourself with it. It is important to be sensitive to your first impressions of the song. What happened as you made your first contact with the words and melody? What sensations and feelings were aroused? What memories evoked? Try to store these impressions away so that you can recall them later when your script starts to take shape.

Now let us analyze the lyrics.

Read the words aloud in a free style and take note of the punctuation pauses and the natural accentuation of the words. Underline words that seem to need emphasis. (I have italicized them according to my judgment; yours may be different.)

Next, sing the song through and observe where the music supports the natural accents and where it does not. For example, "I miss him *so* much" (line 9) has a mutual stress on the word *so*. On the other hand, "When they've been used *so* ill" (line 6) has a verbal stress on *so*, but not a musical one. In such a case, the singer must compensate by somewhat overstressing the word. Generally, however, this particular lyric is well accentuated. Be sure to allow a little space after *Oh yes* (line 2) in order to bring out the comma. Do likewise after *The hell!* (line 15) because the exclamation point needs a little room in order to take effect.

The next to last line presents a particular problem because of the way it is written. Musically, the phrasing needs to be:

I've got to stay true, ju-u-st
As long as he needs me.

Just is a long, climactic note, and it needs to be held. However, as it stands, the phrase makes no sense grammatically. To do that, the comma after *true* must be observed, and *just* must be connected to the following line. There are several solutions, both compromises. The breathing capacities of the singer will be a factor in the choice.

[2]"As Long As He Needs Me." From the Columbia Pictures-Romulus film *Oliver!* Words and Music by Lionel Bart. Copyright ©1960 Lakeview Music Co. Ltd., London, England. TRO—Hollis Music, Inc., New York, controls all publication rights for the U.S.A. and Canada. Used by permission.

1. "I've got to stay true, (catch breath) ju-u-st As long as he needs (breath) me." (The breath before the last word is a concession to the need for air.)
2. "I've got to stay true (space, but no breath) ju-u-st (breath) As long as he needs (breath) me."

Of course, if the singer can dispense with the breath, before *me,* so much the better.

Having gained a cursory acquaintance with the lyrics, now make up your own version, either by speaking or writing. In your own, everyday language and using the first person, retell the lyric in whatever way is natural and easy for you. Do not demand literary excellence of yourself and avoid pretentiousness. If you find it difficult to begin, start by using the first few lines of the lyric and then continue with your own words.

As you retell the lyric, pay attention to internal responses, such as physical sensations or mental images, that may surface. (Incidentally, there is one use of metaphoric language in the lyric that is worth noting: "But all the same I'll play the game his way." The viewpoint that life is a game and that someone else makes up the rules tells much about the character of the singer. The imagination can enlarge on this image: life is a dice game, a roulette wheel, or the Fates spinning the threads of life. What part do *you* play in this game?)

Assuming that you have learned the melody sufficiently to know the notes and rhythms, sing the song through a number of times. At this stage be careful not to do too much at one time. It's best to work on each element separately. For example, sing it through once, paying attention *only* to punctuation and its connection with breathing. Sing it the next time concentrating *only* on note values. In this way, each element can be examined with much greater thoroughness than if they were all lumped together. The integration of the various parts will come later.

The next step is to note the feelings that underlie the words and to give a name to those feelings. Following are some descriptive words that the lyrics suggest:

Lines 1 through 4: defensive and desperate
Lines 5 through 8: pleading for understanding

Note especially where a change of feeling or mood occurs. For instance, in the first interlude (lines 17 and 18), both the words and the music become more restrained and low-keyed. The feeling might be described as rue or regretful. On the next two lines (19 and 20), there is again a change to defiant. Note these words on your vocal score and use them as reminders.

In Chapter 6, three distinct techniques for evoking emotions were discussed: identification, emotional recall and physicalization. Let us now apply each of these and explore our own emotional contact with the subject matter of the lyrics.

Identification: In what ways can you identify with the theme of the lyric? Do you strongly feel the need to be needed? If not, do you perhaps have another need that is comparable in intensity, perhaps an uncommonly strong sense of duty or loyalty toward someone? Can you identify with the loneliness, sadness, defiance, and anger that the text implies? Each point of contact will bring you closer to the song and make it more meaningful. Keep in touch with the identification as you perform the song.

Emotional Recall: Now search your past life for a time when you experienced feelings similar to the ones expressed in the song. Was there a time when you needed a particular friend so desperately that you would have done anything to preserve that friendship? Had you ever taken abuse for the sake of holding on to a loved one? If you have, relive that time. Recall all the details of sights and sounds and odors, all the trivial impressions that were connected with the events. Above all, remember *how you felt* as you sing.

Physicalization: The third way of eliciting emotion is to find a physical attitude, gesture, or movement that symbolizes it. This method may at first glance seem to be mechanical and contrived, but remember it is a means to an end and used only as a catalyst to activate the feelings. Once these have surfaced and are brought to awareness, the physical aspects of the exercise can be dropped. The physicalization, incidentally, should be accompanied by some appropriate words, since the interaction of body and mind is essential.

Referring back to our model, take one of the descriptive words that characterizes the feelings and give it a physical interpretation. Following are some possibilities, but you should invent your own.

four lines of the song express strong feelings of defensive-
ration. Note especially the implication of "in spite of what
eone seems to be telling you to go away and save yourself
situation. However, you refuse and intend to stay on
steadfastly.

To physicalize this situation, brace your legs and tighten your body
as if someone were trying to push you away or drag you from a dangerous
place to safety. Use your arms as if to oppose that person and shake your
head violently in protest. This should be accompanied by some improvised
words, such as: "No, no, I won't go; I won't leave him. He needs me."
These words and body movements should be extremely unrestrained. It
would be even more effective if you could do this exercise with another
actor. Have him try to pull you to safety as you struggle fiercely.

Observe the effect this exercise has had on you. You may find
yourself flooded with feelings. Although you may be somewhat breathless
and spent, nevertheless perform the song, allowing your stirred-up feelings
to spontaneously express themselves.

THE SETTING

At this point, certain elements of meaning and feeling are becoming
apparent. Especially strong are the feelings of love and defiance that the
singer experiences. Beneath it all one senses a half-expressed plea for
understanding and sympathy. The plea seems to be directed at the world in
general. It could also be directed at a particular person.

And where is this all taking place? Wherever the singer chooses. In
reality, of course, she stands alone on a little platform, microphone in
hand, facing a vague blur of people.

As in a film, the scene fades and dissolves into another setting. As
always, the lyric is the source from which the choices should be made. The
setting must not only be plausible, but interesting as well. The atmosphere
it creates must be in keeping with the mood of the song. In the performance
situation, the setting should be pictured in the performer's mind as soon as
the introduction of the song begins and continued throughout the song.

We will now write a brief description of the scene in which the song
takes place. Include the time of day or night, the place, and the general
atmosphere that pervades the scene. Following are two contrasting settings
for "As Long As He Needs Me"

Setting A: A neighborhood bar. It is 2:00 A.M. The air reeks of smoke and liquor. There is a full-length mirror that runs all along the back of the bar. The bartender is at the other end of the bar, trying to get a drunk to go home. Two men in their thirties are sitting at a table in the corner, talking in subdued tones. You are with your best friend. You've had a few drinks, but scarcely feel them.

Setting B: An old brownstone in the West Eighties of New York City. There is a flight of stone steps that leads up to the stoop. The living room of your apartment faces the street. It is five o'clock in the evening. Through the closed windows you can hear the sounds of children playing and taxicabs jolting over the potholes in the street. You look around the room and its meager furnishings: the posters of musical concerts on the wall, the bookcase improvised of milk cartons, and the bed with its faded green spread. You are alone.

THE CHARACTER

A script must be peopled with characters through whom the action of the play unfolds. One of these is the protagonist, whose predicament is central to the story. Of necessity, the singer becomes that protagonist. Who this person is and what traits she exhibits will determine her behavior (performance). These traits are not to be assigned arbitrarily, but must be justified by the lyrics.

The amount of information a lyric divulges about a character will vary greatly. Some will contain many clues regarding the personality of the character/singer, and others will give only the barest hints. As a general rule, the less information the lyric supplies, the more the singer must fill the gaps with her invention.

We will now draw a thumbnail character profile of the character/singer based on the contents of the lyrics.

On one side of a piece of paper write out the lyric as it appears on the sheet music. On the opposite side note any character traits that seem to be implied by the words. These extrapolations should be expressed in the first person and should be the singer's personal reactions to the lyric.

Excerpts from the Lyrics	*Character Profile (sample)*
As long as he needs me Oh yes, he does need me. In spite of what you see I'm sure that he needs me.	I stand by people who need me. (I'm protective.)
Who else would love him still When they've been used so ill ...	I'll take any abuse as long as I'm needed. (I don't think much of myself.)
I miss him so much When he is gone. But when he's near me I don't let on.	It's hard for me to show my feelings.
The way I feel inside, The love I have to hide, The hell! I've got my pride As long as he needs me.	I'm proud. My suffering makes me proud.
He doesn't say the things he should. He acts the way he thinks he should. ...	I know that I settle for very little.
If you are lonely Then you will know When someone needs you You love them so.	I'm lonely. I don't know how to make friends or how to let people approach me. He's the only one who has ever made me feel needed.
I won't betray his trust, Though people say I must. I've got to stay true, just As long as he needs me.[2]	I don't care what he's done to me or anybody else. I defy all.

Compare this profile with your own character, noting similarities and differences. You may relate to some of the traits quite easily, even though others will seem foreign to you. Suppose that the most difficult quality for you to relate to is taking abuse for the sake of love. Try to remember if there was ever a time in your past life when you *did* take abuse (physical or psychological) because you needed to be accepted or loved. If you can't find an appropriate memory, try to imagine what it would be like to be this kind of person. How would you feel and act? How would you justify yourself? Review the exercises on the use of supposition, emotional recall, and improvised role-playing in Chapters 5 and 6.

THE LEAD-IN

So far in our scripting of "As Long As He Needs Me" we have done the following:

- Examined the lyrics for content, both literal and figurative.
- Determined the emotional tone of the song.
- Imagined a locale where the song takes place.
- Assigned particular character traits to the character/singer.

Next we will place the song in a time continuum. Rather than treating it as an event in isolation, the song will be considered part of a chain of cause and effect. In other words, we will presume that some happening, thought, or memory preceded the song and prompted it. In effect, we will devise a short scene that will act as a *lead-in* to the song. The term is used in musical theater to designate the dialogue that immediately precedes a song.

For example, in *Carousel,* the lead-in to the song "You'll Never Walk Alone" is a short section of dialogue during which Nettie, a compassionate, warm-hearted woman, tries to comfort Julie, who is grieving the death of her husband. Thus, the song functions as a response to what has happened and, continues the chain of events leading to the next set of circumstances.

Now for the application. We will treat the song *as if* it emerged from a script. If the song is a popular one, we will invent a lead-in. In order to make these lead-ins more realistic, you may enlist the help of a friend to improvise the dialogue with you, or read it aloud. If the song comes from a musical, as our model does, we have the option of using the original lead-in or creating a new one. We will choose to create a new one.

First, *think of the lyric as a response to something that has preceded it.* Something has happened; someone has said something; you are thinking about a recent or past event. Then, working backward from the first line of the lyric, ask yourself these questions and consider these possible answers:

Questions	*Possible Answers*
What has happened? What am I responding to?	My lover has unjustly accused me of being unfaithful. In fact, he is trying to cover up his own infidelity.

Questions	*Possible Answers*
What reason do I have for saying (singing) "As Long As He Needs Me?"	My best friend has just told me that I'm a fool to put up wtih his abuse for so long.
Am I talking to a person or am I soliloquizing, thinking, remembering, fantasizing?	I'm talking with my confidential friend (be specific).
How am I feeling about what is going on?	I feel both the need to justify myself and to cover up the inner feeling of helplessness about my situation.

Write out in dialogue form a brief scene based on the above material. The last line of the dialogue should lead logically into the first line of the song.

Your friend: "Why do you hang around that guy? He treats you like dirt and you keep coming back for more."

You: "He's not always like that. At times he can be so wonderful. Why, just last week he. . . ."

Your friend: "Why are you defending him? Why do you take all that abuse?"

You: "I'm not sure if I can tell you so you'll understand. But I do know that (sing) as long as he needs me. . . ."

Under performance conditions, of course, this dialogue remains unspoken. It is used only as a mental preparation for the song. While the introduction is being played—which is usually an interval of dead space—imagine the lead-in going on in your mind so that you can smoothly ease into the first line of the lyric. In a similar manner, any musical interlude that occurs in a song, such as an orchestral section or a modulation, should be filled by the performer with relevant thoughts.

As another example, consider "A Foggy Day"

I was a stranger in the city.
Out of town were the people I knew.
I had that feeling of self-pity,
What to do? What to do? What to do?
The outlook was decidedly blue.
But as I walked through the foggy streets alone,
It turned out to be the luckiest day I've known.
A foggy day in London Town
Had me low and had me down.[3]

Questions	*Possible Answers*
What has happened?	I have just received a letter from someone I knew a long time ago.
What reason do I have for saying (singing) "I was a stranger in the city"?	My roommate has questioned me about who the letter is from.
Who am I talking to?	I am talking to a close friend.
How am I feeling about what is going on?	I am experiencing pleasant memories about someone I cared for in the past.

Lead-in

Friend: "You're practically devouring that letter—must be from someone *very* interesting."

You: "You're right, and what a surprise to hear from her after all this time. She was quite a girl. Such memories come back as I'm reading this; I had forgotten what a wonderful place London was in those days."

Friend: "Tell me about it."

You: "Well, (sing) I was a stranger in the city. . . . "

THE AUDIENCE

The relationship between the performer and the audience in nightclubs is obviously quite different than in either musical theater or straight drama. To begin with, there is no attempt to create an illusion of time or place. There is no scenery, few if any props, and the performer is dressed in the current fashion or in some stylized manner. A small spotlight illuminating him may be the only concession to theatricality. The nightclub stage is what it is, nothing else.

The audience, which is often only inches away from the performer, also comes with no expectations of illusion or theatrical magic. It comes to be entertained. It also comes for food and drink and conviviality. The general environment is social rather than cultural, and the atmosphere is one of excitement and gaiety.

It is a difficult place in which to perform. However, the immediacy of contact with the audience and the unpredictability of its moods can also be a source of great stimulation and excitement. The volatility of the situation forces the performer to sharpen responses and constantly adjust to changing conditions.

Another significant difference between the two media is that in the theater the performer assumes a role or character, but in nightclubs he invariably remains himself—a singer performing for an audience. Nevertheless, there are options that are open to him. *In his mind* he can make any number of transformations that are suitable to his purpose. One of these options is to create a script for his song, as has been detailed in previous pages. The script answers questions regarding who the singer is, where he is, and why he says what he says. Another option is his choice of relationship with the audience. He can relate to them as a group of people who have come to enjoy a performance, or by means of his imagination and script, he can incorporate them into participants of his drama.

His choice will depend on the nature of the lyric and its adjustability to his script. Two basic categories of lyrics are to be considered (1) universal subjects and (2) intimate subjects.

The first of these comprises lyrics that express *general* observations about life, people, and places. Universal subjects lend themselves easily to being shared directly with an audience. Examples of such lyrics are:

"Anything Goes" (Cole Porter)
"Cabaret" (Kander and Ebb)
"Oklahoma" (Rodgers and Hammerstein)

Such songs seem to imply an implicit agreement between performer and audiences, as if to say:

"Isn't it crazy how. . . . '
"Don't you agree that. . . . "
"I'm glad that we all feel that. . . . "

Another type of lyric that can be shared directly with the audience is that which has the quality of speech-making, lecturing, or sermonizing. Lyrics that carry a message or philosophy also fit into this category.

"Comedy Tonight" (Sondheim): Announcement
"You Gotta Have Heart" (Adler and Ross): Lecturing
"On That Great Come-And-Get-It Day" (Arlen and Harburg): Sermonizing
"Climb Ev'ry Mountain" (Rodgers and Hammerstein): Spiritual message
"As Time Goes By" (Hupfeld): Philosophy

The following are examples of narrative lyrics:

"Johnny One-Note" (Rodgers and Hart)
"The Trolley Song" (Hugh Martin and Ralph Blane)
"The Gambler" (D. Schlitz) (Much country-western music consists of storytelling and is suitable to the direct approach.)

When it comes to comedy lyrics, humor often has the quality of sharing a confidence with the audience and therefore lends itself well to a direct relating with the audience.

"The Miller's Son" (Sondheim)
"I Cain't Say No" (Rodgers and Hammerstein)
"Second Hand Rose" (Hanley and Clarke)
"Nothing" (Hamlish and Kleban)
"If I Were A Rich Man" (Bock and Harnick)

When performing songs that can be considered period pieces, the performer is either indulging in nostalgia or poking fun at earlier styles of music and sharing this with the audience. The attitude often seems to say: "Didn't they write silly songs in those days and don't we do it much better now?"

Any period from sixteenth-century madrigals to 1950s rock and roll can be presented with the direct appraoch. A few examples follow:

The Gay Nineties	"A Bicycle Built for Two"
The 1920s	"The Varsity Drag"

Songs from film musicals of the 1930s and 1940s	"42nd Street" "Let's Call the Whole Thing Off" "Cheek to Cheek" "Lullaby of Broadway"
1950s Rock and Roll	"Rock Around the Clock" "Love Me Tender" "Why Was I Born Too Late?"

Although the audience is directly addressed in this category of songs, eye contact with any member of the audience close by should be avoided. It is an embarrassment to be singled out and sung to. Also to be avoided is the practice of fixing the eyes on a spot on the wall or the floor and singing to it. Such artifices betray the performer's insecurity and lack of concentration.

In the second category, in which feelings of intimacy are expressed, the intimacy may be of the sort that is shared by friends, lovers, or any two people who are close to each other. It may also take the form of a soliloquy—the speaking (or singing) of one's thoughts, memories, and fantasies.

The relationship between performer and audience in such songs is indirect. The performer behaves as though he were in a situation of intimacy with another person, or as if he were alone. Although he faces the audience, he does not acknowledge it. His vision is turned inward and what he *sees* are the mental images that occupy his mind. Such inward *seeing* can be easily observed, since it is reflected in the performer's eye movements and facial expressions.

When the performer is seemingly unaware of the audience while focusing on inner images he is in a state of *dual attention*. His primary focus is on the subject matter of the song and his personal involvement with it. In his imagination he is living out the details of his script. His secondary attention, however, is on the audience. Though he seems to be oblivious of its presence, he maintains continuous contact with it. He hears its laughter, the snatches of conversation, the silences. He is aware of its moods of excitement or boredom. He *sees* very little, perhaps a blur of people, since his concentration is inward.

He responds to all such feedback and uses it to orient himself and adjust his performance. Thus, if he is singing a comedy song and people are not laughing, it may be that they cannot hear clearly. His self-correction may be to improve his diction. (Of course, the problem is that the material is poor, in which case diction will not help.) If he senses that their attention is diffused, he will need to sharpen his own concentration and energy. If, on the other hand, he is aware of a concentrated silence that reaches out toward him, he knows that he is doing well and that the audience is in his hands.

The following are songs that require inner focus:

"My Funny Valentine" (Rodgers and Hart)
"Soon It's Gonna Rain" (Jones and Schmidt)
"Who Can I Turn To" (Bricusse and Newley)
"Pieces of Dreams" (Bergman and Legrand)
"Alfie" (David and Bacharach)
"As Long As He Needs Me" (Bart)
"Send In The Clowns" (Sondheim)
"What Kind Of Fool Am I?" (Bricusse and Newley)
"Over the Rainbow" (Harburg and Arlen)
"I've Grown Accustomed To Her Face" (Lerner and Loewe)

A general comment regarding audiences: Two attitude extremes are to be avoided by the performer. The first is completely ignoring the audience, and the second is being preoccupied by it. In the first case, the performer is isolated and has put himself in a glass cage to be observed. However, without reaching out with his personal energy and making contact, there is no communication. The audience will sense this, feel excluded, and become either resentful or apathetic.

In the second case, concentration and involvement are impossible for the performer because the focus of attention is completely outward. The audience sees none of the performers feelings except, perhaps, the anxiety to succeed. Such overattention to the audience is a major factor in causing stage fright, a nightmare from which many performers suffer. When this happens, the audience becomes transformed into a collection of critics and judges who are out to "get" the performer. The problems of performance anxieties and techniques for dealing with them are discussed at greater length in Appendix C.

To sum up, although the performer's awareness of the audience is constant, the degree of awareness is in a continual state of flux. It will vary from the subliminal to the highly conscious. A comparison might be made with a multichannel sound recording. There is a separate channel for lyrical content, emotional content, vocal interpretation, movement, audience awareness, and so on. Although all these channels are projected simultaneously, they are never experienced with equal intensity. There is a constant changing of sound levels, and the prominence of one over the other depends on whatever quality needs to be dominant at any particular moment. The performer's skill and intuition guides these elements into an appropriate balance.

THE MUSICAL ARRANGEMENT

The final step in our scripting process is to give the song a musical structure and style. This will determine how long the piece will be and how many choruses, interludes, modulations, and other extensions it will comprise. It will set the song in a particular musical idiom, such as jazz, rock, Latin-American, conventional musical theater style, or a mix of any of these. It will also determine tempos, musical textures, instrumentation (whether the accompaniment will consist of a keyboard instrument, guitar, or orchestra), and it will contain musical ideas, configurations, and motifs that will give it an individual character. All these things put together are called the musical arrangement.

Before we get back to our model song, a brief explanation concerning the craft of musical arranging is necessary in order to acquaint the performer with the choices this entails and how these choices can affect the script we have been developing.

A simple way of demonstrating what an arrangement is and what it does is to compare the sheet music of a song with a recorded version (or better yet, several versions) of the same song.

The sheet music (or song sheet) is the original source material from which the singer learns the words and music. It also provides a piano accompaniment. Aside from such information as title, names of composers, and publisher, it consists of three staves of music—the top stave being the vocal line with the lyrics printed below, the bottom two staves making up the piano accompaniment. There is, in addition, a set of chord symbols written above the top stave. These are a kind of musical shorthand, indicating the harmonies. They are useful because they give the pianist or guitarist a means of improvising an accompaniment without having to read the piano part note by note.

Most vocal scores for shows do not contain chord symbols because the piano parts are more complete than for pop sheet music and are intended to be played literally. However, shows with a contemporary flavor, such as *A Chorus Line* and *The Wiz,* do include chord symbols in their scores.

Since song sheets are primarily intended for the general public, a typical piano part is most often rudimentary, consisting generally of a single line for the right hand, interspersed with a few chords. The left hand is given a simple bass part. However, piano-vocals that are quite sophisticated and require a good pianist are also found.

If you listen to a recording of the same piece of music and compare the two, there are a great number of discrepancies between what one hears and sees. For example, the key in which the piece is sung on the recording may be different from that of the sheet music. In fact, there may be several changes of key. The sequence of parts (the verses and choruses) may be rearranged or edited, and the style of accompaniment may not at all resemble that of the print. Even the basic time signature may be changed from say, 4/4 to 3/4. Another difference will be due to the fact that the singer on the recording is backed up by an instrumental group, giving the arrangement a particular sound and style and utilizing the sound-modification techniques that are common in recordings. Lastly, the singer on the recording often alters the notes of the song with embellishments and improvisations that are not to be found in the printed music.

All in all, the comparison between the two versions clearly points out that the recording artist, with the help of his arranger, has altered the original song in significant ways. The degree of alteration may vary from slight to drastic.

Two examples of recordings will illustrate the extremes: The first is Barbra Streisand's "The Way We Were" (Columbia Records). This recording follows the sheet music version fairly closely. The key in both is A major. The basic piano figure used in the recording is the same as is written in the introduction of the printed music. The routine (with one exception) is the same. The exception consists of an addition on the record of eight bars of the melody prior to the song proper. These eight bars are sung without words, on the vowel *oo*. They provide an atmospheric introduction to the main body of the song. The same device is used at the end of the record, creating a unity between beginning and end. Instrumentally, the arrangement is simple and uncluttered. It begins with piano alone. The strings are gradually introduced and come to a climax seven bars before the end. From this point on, the intensity that has been building up subsides, and the song fades softly to the end. Incidentally, at the climactic point just mentioned, Streisand for the first time alters the written melody by choosing a higher note on "whenev*er*," then sliding down back to the original tune. The arrangement is a faithful representation of the lyrics and music, creating a mood of nostalgia and regret which is in keeping with the singer's interpretation.

By comparison, Judy Garland's arrangement of "Come Rain or Come Shine" (*Judy at Carnegie Hall*—Capitol Records) is a study in extreme contrasts. The song, one of Harold Arlen's best, is a strong blues-style ballad, usually performed in a moderately slow tempo.

The original key (F major, ending in d minor) has been lowered in the recording to B♭ major and, through a series of modulations, ends in the key of a minor (which enables her to finish on a high C in chest register).

The arrangement begins with a Latin feel: bongos playing in a very fast cut-time tempo. The first eight bars are sung with bongos as the only accompaniment. On the ninth bar, a syncopated bass figure (still in the Latin idiom) is introduced. This continues until the middle of the chorus. Then the feel changes to 4/4 jazz played with an exciting big-band sound. Throughout the arrangement, bars are added to extend phrases, and phrases are repeated in modulating patterns.

The second chorus continues in the jazz idiom, but now the tempo is again fast with the brass and saxes providing exciting fills. At times there are abrupt, unexpected stops in the rhythm that suspend the listener in surprise, continuing again, more frenetic than before. The drums throughout are dominant, supporting the band figures and filling in the ends of phrases. The arrangement finally comes to a screeching halt with both singer and band at the very top of their registers, having exhausted practically every device for creating musical excitement.

To try to evaluate an arrangement such as this in terms of singing/acting would be meaningless, since it obviously is not intended to be an acting piece, but a show piece, a *tour de force* that will sweep an audience off its feet. Although unquestionably Judy Garland sings it with much feeling and energy, the arrangement, in the author's opinion, goes a bit too far in its attempt at originality and eventually draws attention to itself at the expense of the singer. Nevertheless, it demonstrates how far it is possible to stray from the printed page in transmuting the source material into an arrangement.

Arranging is a very specialized skill that requires years of training to perfect, and no performer can be expected to orchestrate and write out the instrumental parts of his pieces. However, there are two separate elements to the craft: There is the technical side—the harmony, counterpoint, and orchestration. These are the skills that are presumably beyond the singer's capabilities. Then there is the more creative side to arranging, conceiving the general mood or character of the piece, the musical idiom that is employed, the shape of the arrangement, and unifying devices such as the one used in "The Way We Were." Often an idea will be triggered by an image in the lyric as, for instance, "restless as a willow." It is easy to see how this could generate a particular form of accompaniment.

If the singer has learned to listen well to the recordings of all kinds of music and has come to recognize the contribution that the arranger makes in each case, original ideas will emerge when she works on a new piece. She will find that it becomes easier and easier to think creatively in musical terms, and the arrangements will more truly represent her personality and concepts.

Having selected an arranger who will actually write the musical arrangement, it is important that the details of your script be thoroughly discussed with him so that there is a consensus on all musical matters and the arrangement carries out its part of the interpretation of the song. Without being given very specific instructions regarding musical style the average arranger (assuming that he knows his craft) will come up with an arrangement that will probably sound "effective," meaning that it will be commercially stereotyped. It may also introduce musical ideas that will be irrelevant or contradictory to your intentions. Hence the importance of a careful and detailed collaboration.

A good arrangement should serve both the song and the singer. It should have a definite attitude. If the singer has conceived a script for the song, the arrangement should fit its general mood.

In working out the ideas for an arrangement, time should be allowed for experimentation. It is difficult to predict whether or not an arrangement is successful without an audience reaction. If it does not work, it will need to be reexamined and reworked. Sometimes an arrangement is too long and cannot keep the interest of the audience, or the ending will be wrong or too abrupt and ruin an otherwise good arrangement. An audience must be forewarned of the approach of the finish so that it can prepare itself to respond. Sometimes the orchestral finish over the last note will be too extended and kill the applause. The arrangement may be too complicated, change keys too often, try too hard to be interesting, and so on. Trial and error are unavoidable, and experience will hopefully guide the performer to the right solution.

Following are some specific points to consider in working out an arrangement:

The General Musical Idiom: The deciding factor should be the appropriateness of the idiom. Does it fit the conception of the song? For example, if we were to try to put a hard rock background to our model, "As Long As He Needs Me," the strong rhythmic element would contradict the dramatic nature of the lyric. How would a light rock beat affect the song? It might work if the continuity of the beat were broken up with some kind of contrast, for instance, doing the interlude in ad lib fashion. The conventional idiom in which the song was treated in the musical might also be considered a possibility.

The Introduction: Does the song need an introduction or will an arpeggio or a key-note suffice? Factors to be considered are: Will the performer be coming on stage during the introduction or will she already be on stage? What kind of number has preceded the song? How much time will the performer need to get into the mood of the song?

The introduction should set the tone of what is to follow. While it is being played, the singer should be visualizing the setting and the circumstances of her script.

The Key: The key selected for this song should be the lowest that can comfortably be sung. It should be low because of the dark quality of the lyric and also because we will want to climb into higher keys as the arrangement progresses. This means that the ending key and notes have to be kept in mind in planning the sequence of keys. However, the choice cannot be fully made until the length of the arrangement and the routine (the sequence of parts) have been decided on. If the performer has a low chest register, the starting key would probably be in the neighborhood of F major.

Length and Routine: The length of an arrangement depends on how long it can maintain the interest of the audience. This, in turn, is related to the strength of the performance as well as the imagination and creativity of the arranger.

Regarding routine, several possibilities present themselves. Let us first examine the routine that was used in the original musical, *Oliver.*

A one-bar orchestral introduction.

The first chorus (key of F).

Interlude ("He doesn't say the things he should").

The second chorus. The last eight bars of this are lifted into the key of A♭, providing a powerful and climactic ending to the song.

The orchestral tag is brief, consisting of only one bar of strongly punctuating chords.

Although this is a perfectly sound routine, let us see what other options may be equally usable. For example:

A four-bar introduction based on thematic material. Let us make this nonrhythmic, perhaps atmospheric chords, to set the mood of the piece. (The key is F.)

Interlude. This can be done in ad lib fashion to the accompaniment of a single instrument, say piano.

First chorus. A light rock background that does not intrude on the lyrics and allows the singer to phrase freely.

Second interlude. A second set of lyrics to be found on page 123 of the vocal score of *Oliver* can be used.

This interlude may also be sung ad lib (perhaps accompanied by guitar this time).

On the last chord of this interlude, the back-up group can provide a modulating chord (Am7/D) while the singer takes the pick-up notes into the next chorus in the key of G (the common note, G connects the two keys).

We are now into the second chorus (key of G). On the words "I won't betray his trust," we can modulate once more, going up another half step into the key of A♭ and ending in a big finish.

The orchestral tag can be lengthened to two bars.

In selecting these keys, the assumption is that the performer has a good high C in the chest register. But if, for instance, she can only reach a B♭ in chest, other options are available: (1) The whole arrangement can be transposed one tone down. It would need a very low voice to manage that. (2) The last high note can be altered so that instead of singing a C on the word "needs," a B♭ is substituted (which is almost as good).

It is important in selecting keys that the performer avoid exposure to a register that she cannot easily handle. It is better to have the body of the arrangement in a comfortable key, even if a high note at the end must be sacrificed, than to sing in a key that is too low for the sake of that last high note.

The Instrumental Setting: Unfortunately, the performer in a nightclub has little say about the instrumental accompaniment that will serve her. It is rare to see an orchestra of more than five or six musicians playing for a show; more likely, it will be a trio or even a single accompanist. Practically the only place in the country where big show orchestras are still employed is Las Vegas. So the question of instrumentation is largely academic, and the performer's "charts" will most often be written out for a rhythm section plus several lead instruments such as trumpet and sax.

The Shape of the Arrangement: This is the general distribution of energy and the placement of the climax in an arrangement. For example, the arrangement of "The Way We Were" is in the shape of an arch. It starts quietly, gradually gathering energy, and peaking seven bars from the end. From there on it descends, returning to the calmness of the beginning. This arch-like construction is commonly used, since it has the advantage of a built-in unity, ending as it begins.

Another shape is typified by the arrangement of "As Long As He Needs Me." In this instance, starting from a low point, there is a gradual rise in intensity up to the very end of the piece, the climax occurring simultaneously with the last chord. This shape resembles the steep ascent up a mountain to the very peak. As in mountain climbing, the upward direction may occasionally be broken up by a temporary level or downward movement, the climb being then resumed.

Yet another shape, exemplified by the Judy Garland recording previously discussed, starts at a high level of excitement and stays there throughout. The shape is of a high plateau that has occasional dips, but basically stays at that high level. This shape can be problematic, since it is difficult to maintain high energy without being alleviated somehow. The arranger has been aware of this and has accordingly introduced various changes of tempo and style. He has also reserved some energy before the end so that there could be a final upward surge. This arrangement also illustrates the powerful effect that the repetition of a phrase can produce; especially in fast numbers. Note the reinforcing and exciting threefold repetition of "I'm gonna love you," accompanied each time with a rising key change, before the final "Come rain or come shine."

These three are the most basic shapes for arrangements. Although others are possible, they are usually variations of one of these. The contents of the lyrics should determine which arrangement is chosen. Also to be considered are the intentions of the performer regarding entertainment values versus acting values. There is a great temptation for the performer in nightclubs to play down to the public and believe that her standards must be lowered in order to gain acceptance. This mistaken belief has been disproved by many great nightclub performers. The singing actor can always be true to the song regardless of whether the context is a musical theater stage, a nightclub, or any other musical setting.

The following exercise tests the appropriateness of the musical treatment of a song.

Exercise

Take a standard ballad like "My Funny Valentine" and have your pianist apply various types of accompaniment to it—for instance, a light rock background or a tinkly eighth-note piano figure. Which of these seems to best fit your overall concept of the song?

Experiment with an up-tune like "Luck, Be A Lady Tonight" (*Guys and Dolls*) and notice the effect of a fast jazz tempo or a heavy rock beat in half time. You may find that by changing the accompaniment, the mood and atmosphere of the song is also influenced. A jazz beat applied to a song that has a heavy, dramatic lyric may detract from this quality, whereas it would add an appropriate joyfulness to a more light-hearted lyric. A conventional accompaniment goes well with a ballad but not in a fast number that needs a lot of excitement. Become aware of the power of the musical idiom to influence and modify elements of character, emotion, and energy.

Experiment with tempos in the same way, noticing how different tempos affect the mood of a song, and how your own reactions to the song will vary accordingly.

THE SINGING ACTOR

This book began with a brief look at the field of musical theater as it is today, of the extraordinary diversity in both theatrical forms and performance styles, of the difficulties both student performers and professionals experience in trying to meet the multiplicities of demands, and the issue of acquiring training in this field.

One thing that seems clear from even a hasty look at contemporary musicals is that the performer is expected to be able to express himself in many modes of performance. In addition to the basics of singing, dancing, and acting he may be required to do any number of specialties, from puppeteering and pantomime to acrobatics or swordsmanship. This is not to say that all these skills are required of all performers, but that the performer whose repertoire of skills is largest is most employable.

However, singing, dancing, and acting are the major skills the performer needs since without them he cannot successfully compete in the profession. (Although the subject of dancing is not in the domain of the author's expertise, its importance to the musical theater performer is, of course, equal to that of singing and acting.)

Anyone who is serious about a career in musical theater and respects it as a legitimate art form realizes that he must acquire a solid foundation in these disciplines and expect to devote years of study to that end. Formal training in singing, acting, and dancing is usually acquired in private schools of performance studies or in university programs. This book is certainly not intended to be either a substitute or a shortcut for such training, but it is meant to help the performer correlate his skills and offer ways of refining his craft.

Basic vocal training must continue throughout the career of the performer so that the voice has quality, flexibility, and the capability of singing difficult music without self-damage. (Ironically, it is on the lower rungs of the professional ladder that the demands for vocal excellence are greatest. As one ascends to the rarified regions of stardom, vocal demands are often relaxed, and acting, personality, and reputation take precedence.) As musical theater has become more action-oriented, the singing actor has had greater choreographic demands on him than ever before. This trend in musicals closely parallels that in action films and television shows where visual and aural effects are piled one on top of the other without relief. The consequence of this trend is that the singer is also expected to be a dancer. During the casting of a musical, singing auditions are invariably followed by dance auditions where a high degree of proficiency is expected.

One particular development has had an enormous effect on the singer-dancer amalgamation. That is the increasing practice of prerecording voice-tracks, which are then played during choreographed numbers. As a consequence, the singer-dancer, freed from the microphone and not having to conserve physical energy in order to sing, merely lip-syncs to the voice-track and is able to dance quite intricate routines without loss of voice quality or volume.

Acting in musical theater also has special traits that distinguish it from straight plays. The reason for the difference is found in the genesis of musical scripts. In almost every instance, a musical script comes into being through adaptation, usually from a novel, short story, or play. In the process of condensation, a 500 page novel may get whittled down to a script that has a playing time of perhaps an hour and a quarter, with the rest of the time reserved for musical numbers. Such surgery obviously entails the cutting of many details of plot and character development. The telescoping of events and the rapid pace that result from the adaptation have their effect on the singing actor. There is little time for dwelling on pregnant pauses or slow transitions. All must be done with great directness and briskness of tempo.

Since the scenes are usually brief, the singing actor must use the musical numbers to fill gaps that the script leaves open, getting maximum meaning from the songs and also finding values and character traits that may not be explicitly spelled out in the script. This can be positive or negative, depending on the performer's creativity. If he approaches such limitations with an attitude of challenge, he can often tap unknown reservoirs of imagination.

As the performer trains and gains experience, he gradually develops a sense of what is good and what is not. Criteria are formed based on emulated models, great performers who are admired, either for their vocal brilliance (Barbra Streisand) or their versatility (Angela Lansbury). It is important that these models be realistically appraised, and their good and bad qualities differentiated. Streisand's command of vocal colors is fantastic, as is the evenness of her scale as she goes from her low register through the middle and into the high. On the other hand, her habit of wiggling her jaw sideways definitely does not warrant imitation.

Criteria are also formed by listening to what great performers say about their own work. Books such as *Actors Talk About Acting* or Henry Pleasant's *The Great American Popular Singers* bring us into intimate contact with the thoughts and personal experiences of those artists who have established high standards in their fields.

Nightclub performing, the topic of the last part of the book, is not demeaning work—at least, it need not be. There are nightclub acts that have class and dignity, as well as those that are crass and tasteless. The nightclub performer has many choices open to him, perhaps too many. What I have offered is a structured form that can be creatively used. Using the theatrical scene as a model, the performer constructs an imaginary background for his song. It is a device often used instinctively, for it is based on simple storytelling.

Having a structure also gives the performer a sense of confidence, since he has filled it out according to his own experience. Self-confidence comes when the performer is sure of what he is doing, when he has experienced success and coped with failures. The nightclub performer, standing alone in a spot light, needs especially to feel his competence and strength. His contact with the audience is in a continually fluctuating state. He is interacting with it face to face, addressing it directly, and then retreating into his private world of intimate thoughts and experiences.

The nightclub performer must know his audience's general composition, and expectations, and changing moods, which may swing from apathy to enthusiasm and back again, and use the feedback to monitor his performance and selection of music. This is the field of entertainment where the performer is on his own more than in any other. He needs to know a great deal about programming, costuming, lighting, sound systems, and musical arranging. His self-reliance is constantly being tested by conditions that require him to improvise, adapt to unexpected problems, and still show himself at his best.

A nightclub and musical theater performer must eventually get to the place where he feels competent to be self-directive. The wise stage director trusts the instincts and talents of the singing actor and gives him leeway to express himself in his particular way. But he can only give that trust to the performer who has trust in himself.

One looks for reasons why these qualities of self-trust are so rarely seen, why people seem generally more in touch with their weaknesses and inadequacies than their strengths and assets. The answer may lie in the fact that we live in a service society. Few individuals feel competent to do anything but a few specialized tasks. When other tasks need to be done, a specialist in those fields are called. A dependence on others is created along with an accompanying undermining of self-confidence. Thus, college students depend on career counselors to guide them, and performers hang on every word of their teachers or directors, waiting to be told what to do next.

Teachers are necessary, of course, and the need for rigorous training has been emphasized often enough. But each individual has knowledge that is intuitive, that can discriminate and learn directly from life itself. Our inner promptings are important signs of our personality wanting to emerge and assert itself. And unless these messages are heard and responded to, our technical training will make us merely skilled workers.

Furthermore, without trust in these instinctual urgings, the imagination deteriorates and it becomes difficult to *do* unaccustomed things or even *imagine* doing them. The imagination, which is our one guaranteed freedom and the performer's supreme tool, then withers away through lack of use, much as an unused muscle weakens and finally becomes unresponsive.

The performer works hard at his basic studies. He puts his time in. He must also work hard at himself—to know himself and to work *through* himself. Whatever he learns must go by way of his personal experience, not through anyone else. He learns important lessons while walking down the street or mingling with friends, observing and listening. He learns by sharing his knowledge and experience with others and by asking questions. He learns by having a positive attitude and by realizing the destructive power that resides in negativism. And he learns by daily expanding his awareness of himself and of the world, incorporating his awareness into his formal studies, infusing the skills he is acquiring with his own particular touch so that when he performs, the audience experiences the presence of a unique personality.

Appendix A:
Some Practical
Details

THE CARE OF YOUR MUSIC

It is part of your responsibility as a performer to take the proper care of your music, since the success of your performance will depend, in part, on the manner in which you are accompanied.

- Your music should be written in the right key, regardless of whether it is printed or in manuscript form.
- All markings and corrections should be clear so that your pianist has no difficulty in understanding them. Use a dark, soft pencil so that the markings are easily visible.
- Be sure that the first and second endings are easily distinguished.
- Often *dal segno* signs 𝄋 and *coda* signs ⊕ are printed in such tiny letters that the pianist can easily miss them. They should be boldly circled with a dark pencil so that they are unmistakable.

- Be sure that all previous markings that are no longer valid are completely erased.
- Check to see whether your music stays easily on the piano rack (especially if it is new music that you have never performed in public). Many good performances have been ruined because the poor pianist was struggling to keep his music open and play at the same time. Remember, every time something goes wrong with your accompaniment, it is *your* performance that suffers.

TEMPO MARKINGS

The top of the piano part should have the tempo marked in bold letters. It is best to couple the tempo markings with a word that relates to the style of the accompaniment, together with a reference to the meter of the music, such as *Bright Jazz 4/4, Slow Bossa Nova, Heavy Rock 4, Light Rock Feel,* or *Country-Western Feel.* These descriptive markings are very helpful to the pianist, especially if she has not had the opportunity of rehearsing with you.

TRANSPOSITIONS

The printed vocal scores to musicals are written in the keys that the original performers sang the songs. Thus, in the case of "Hello, Dolly!" all the songs that were sung by Carol Channing are printed in her keys.

In the field of pop music, the printed keys are sometimes those of the recording artist who made the song famous, or the publisher may decide to print the music in a middle-range key that will suit the average singer. Even then, it is rare that the printed key will be the optimum one for you.

Finding the right key for yourself should be done with care, since your choice can make you sound your best or your worst. Experiment a lot before deciding. Here are some factors to consider:

- The general comfort of the key.
- Your vocal strengths and weaknesses. Does the key expose your best notes or your worst?
- Extremes of range. Can you handle the top notes easily? Can you project enough in the lower register of the song?
- The general character of the piece. If the song is a gentle love song, you will want to keep the key in an easy-sounding middle range. if, on the other hand, the song makes a strong statement, you will want a higher key that will bring out its power.

- Whether to use a belting voice or head voice (a choice point for female singers). Consider the kind of sound that is required by the idiom of the song. All of Eliza's songs from *My Fair Lady* are traditionally sung in head voice. We have come to associate the character with a certain vocal sound. If, however, you are singing "Wouldn't It Be Loverly?" in a nightclub, there is no reason why you can't sing it in chest, since the conditions of the stage play do not apply in the present context.
- The climactic high note. Often a choice has to be made between a key that will enable you to sing the high note at the end of the song in the best part of voice, thereby putting the body of the song in too low a register, or selecting one that will be good for most of the song, but rob you of the effective, brilliant last high note. In the author's opinion, one or two high notes should never determine the key of a song, no matter how effective they may be. Usually, with patient rehearsing and trying out different solutions to the problem, an alternate ending can be found that is satisfactory.

ALTERNATIVES TO COMPLETE TRANSPOSITION

Ideally, all your piano parts should be written out in the keys that you want to sing them. This is especially important in cases where the piano part is difficult. It is unrealistic and self-defeating to expect a pianist to be able to transpose your music. Besides, the anxiety of worrying about your accompaniment will certainly interfere with your performance and put you at a disadvantage.

Having your piano parts transposed can run into a bit of money. If you can't afford to give the part completely written out in the proper key, at least have the melody line transposed. In that case, the chord symbols (also transposed, of course) should be written *over* the melody. Partial transposition such as this is a shortcut and by no means as good as the complete job. However, if your pianist is experienced in reading chord symbols, it will probably suffice.

A second, even poorer alternative is for the singer to transpose the chord symbols that are printed over the notes of the sheet music. This will give the pianist at least *some* help in transposing. Thus, for example, if a piece of music is being transposed down a tone from the key of C to the key of B♭, then every chord symbol would be transposed down a tone: G7 would become F7, Ddim. would be Cdim., F9 would be E♭9, and so on.

INSTRUCTING
YOUR ACCOMPANIST

Not only should your music be marked clearly, but your accompanist should be instructed in the manner that you want it to be played. Even if your music is written in the right key, clearly marked, and legible, you should still listen carefully to the accompaniment that is being provided for you and make concrete suggestions regarding your preferences. Much of popular music accompanying depends on the pianist having the right feel for the music. It is rare to find a piano part can be played exactly as written and give the proper musical support. It is very important for the pianist to know specifically what you want of him.

Aside from directions relating to tempo, try to convey the feeling you want the accompaniment to have. Such comments as "play it with a rock beat," or "give me more rhythmic support," or "just play sustained chords for these eight bars" are understandable instructions for an experienced pianist. References to the style of a particular performer or of a particular recorded version of a song can further clarify what you require in your accompaniment.

CHANGING
THE ACCOMPANIMENT

One of the most valuable ways that a singer can train himself is to make a study of musical backgrounds. Listen to a Barbra Streisand recording and take notice of what goes on behind the voice. What kind of support is the singer receiving from the orchestra? What are the colors and textures of the instruments? What is happening rhythmically? How about style? How do the various elements in the accompaniment relate to what the singer is doing?

The more the performer becomes aware of the astonishing variety of backgrounds to which a song can be subjected, the more he can learn to shape his own style and thereby become an individual artist, rather than a carbon copy of someone else.

Starting out with the printed music of a particular piece, following are some common changes of accompaniment.

Change of Style: Introducing a different style of accompaniment can dramatically alter the feeling of a piece. For instance, if the original music is written in a neutral ballad style, the substitution of a soft rock background will make for a drastic and perhaps refreshing change of sound. It can be creative fun experimenting with different kinds of backgrounds for a song—jazz, Latin, or soft or hard rock. Select the one that fits into your overall concept of the piece. If your pianist has the flexibility to do so, suggest that he improvise the accompaniment in one of these styles.

Change of Tempo: Sometimes an old song can be rejuvenated by doing it in an unaccustomed tempo. Streisand's version of "Happy Days Are Here Again" is an example of such a treatment. By applying a much slower tempo to this usually brightly paced song, a novel interpretation of the lyric was made possible. Similarly Rodgers and Hart's "Lover," originally a waltz, was successfully transformed into a fast, driving jazz song by Peggy Lee.

The Use of a Recurring Motif: The use of a repeated musical phrase or motif can be a unifying device of great effectiveness. Such a phrase, which is usually short and rhythmic, may serve as an introduction to the song, as an ending, and as a filler to be used at the ends of phrases. "The Man Who Got Away" *(A Star Is Born),* exemplifies this device. The repeated two-bar phrase of the introduction is used throughout the song at strategic points.

The Use of Pastiche: The accompaniment can serve to comment on the lyric by imitating a particular style of music. For example, a section of the arrangement may be made to sound like 1920s ragtime, 1940s swing music, 1950s rock, or any other past musical style. The purpose of the pastiche may be to satirize, make a comedic point, or create an atmosphere of nostalgia.

The Use of Silence: Occasionally a short section of a song can be effectively highlighted by singing it *a capella* (without accompaniment). This may be done in order to point up a "punch line" in a comedy song or to bring into relief a particular word or phrase.

   Stop time is another way of using silence. In stop time every bar is accented with a chord on the down beat. The rest of the bar is left open—

silent. In this way the voice is left in the clear, and the singer is able to express the lyric without interference from the accompaniment. Stop time is most effective in patter-type songs in which there are so many words per bar that they might otherwise be difficult to comprehend.

Accents: Another way of bringing attention to a word or phrase is to accompany it by an unusual sound. Such a sound may be a purposeful dissonance, a sound of extremely high or low range, a sound of unexpected loudness or softness, or the sound of an unusual instrument. In this way the accompaniment either mirrors what the lyric says or comments on it.

Changes of Key Within the Arrangement: An accompaniment can gain much interest and energy through the use of modulations and key changes. To sing more than two choruses of a song in the same key tends generally to become monotonous, and a modulation to another key is advisable. The most common key changes are those that go up a half step. However, any key change can be effective, provided that the modulation is smoothly carried out, and that the new key has a feeling of forward motion.

A clichéd key sequence, but one that is still employed by many top artists, goes as follows:

If the first chorus, for example, is in the key of G, at the end of the chorus go back to the release (middle section) of the song. When you get to the last eight bars, go a half tone higher to the key of Ab and finish in this key.

Due to the greater number of choruses, the proportions are different for faster numbers. For instance, if you were planning to sing three choruses of a fast song, you would have several options: You could start in the key of G, go to the key of Ab on the second chorus, and then go even a half step higher to A on the third chorus. As an alternative, you could sing the first and second chorus in the key of G and then go to Ab for the third chorus. Whatever the sequence of keys, it is always effective (providing that it does not throw your voice out of range) to raise the key of the last eight bars by a half step.

Changing the Ending: Whether to change the ending of a song or to sing it in its original form depends on the individual song. Some songs, especially ballads, need little or no ending changes, for a slowing down of the last few bars is usually sufficient to come to a satisfactory finish. Sometimes repeating the last line of the lyric will serve to finalize the ending more emphatically.

In fast tunes, the effect of slowing down the last phrase can be accomplished by an elongation of the notes, while at the same time maintaining the tempo. An example of the application of this technique is "I Got Rhythm." The last line of the song, "Who could ask for anything more?" is written to four bars of music. By elongating the words *ask for any-thing more,* the four-bar phrase is extended to eight bars. The last note, *more,* is thereby held for four bars, while the orchestra plays a *ride-out* (An instrumental ending played as the singer holds the last note).

Ending on a Higher or Lower Note: Congruency should be the determinant in choosing an ending note. Does a higher note fit the interpretation of the song, or does it suddenly show voice for the sake of voice?

In "The Impossible Dream," the last note, Bb, may be raised to a D, or even an F (provided, of course, that this is vocally feasible). The justification lies in the lyric: "To reach the unreachable star."

On the other hand, the ending of "A Foggy Day" could be sung in the upper or lower octave, depending on whether a joyous or a reflective mood was conceived by the performer.

Repetition of the Final Phrase: Often the final two or four bars of a piece can be repeated. This is especially true of jazz-type pieces, such as "That Old Black Magic" (Mercer and Arlen), "They Can't Take That Away From Me" (George and Ira Gershwin), and "The Lady Is A Tramp" (Rodgers and Hart). The repetitions may be literal or varied in some way, perhaps even changing key. The effect of the repetition is to notify the audience of the approaching end of the song and to create a sense of finality and resolution. There is also an accumulation of energy that results from the repetition which heightens the final impact of a number.

Much can be learned from certain composers about modifications that can transform a song into an arrangement. The printed song sheets of John Kander, for instance, are often complete arrangements. In many of the songs from *Cabaret, Zorba, Chicago, New York, New York,* and other works, he makes consistent use of recurring motifs, tempo and key changes, repetition of phrases, and other devices. The works of Cy Coleman and Stephen Sondheim also offer valuable lessons in this area.

SOURCES FOR REPERTOIRE

The perennial complaint one hears from singers is "I don't know what to sing. Where can I find good material?"

Keep a notebook in which you jot down the names of musical numbers. Make separate categories for different kinds of numbers, and put each category on a separate page. Remember that opening and closing numbers will be the "big" songs that open or close an act. Following is a typical listing.

Opening and Closing Numbers
"Cabaret"
"Applause! Applause!"
"It's Almost Like Being in Love"
"New York, New York"

Ballads
"My Funny Valentine"
"Someone to Watch Over Me"
"The Party's Over"

Narrative Songs
"Have I Stayed Too Long at the Fair?"
"The Trolley Song"
"Johnny One Note"

Blues and Spirituals
"God Bless the Child"
"Stormy Weather"
"Blues in the Night"

Comedy and Character Songs
"I Cain't Say No"
"Raindrops Keep Fallin' on My Head"
"Nothing"

In addition to the above categories, you should have a good representation of contemporary pop songs.

If you play an instrument, tap dance, do impressions, or have any other skill, you should have a number in which you can demonstrate your particular specialty.

For the sake of auditions it is important to have several songs in your repertoire that show your voice at its best. Select songs that have a legato vocal line and that allow you to sustain long notes. Also keep in mind that you will want to show your vocal range. Some examples of songs such as these are as follows:

"All the Things You Are
"So In Love"
"If I Loved You"
"Stranger in Paradise"
"I Could Have Danced All Night"

Most newpapers publish lists of the top current recordings. These come out in the weekend editions. There are also weekly trade papers such as *Variety, Back Stage, Billboard,* and *Cashbox.* The latter two even give a breakdown of popularity according to region.

The variously named Giant, Jumbo, and Encyclopedic collections of songs available in most music stores can also be helpful in selecting a repertoire. Some contain full piano accompaniments, others merely have a single-line melody together with lyrics and chord symbols. A careful perusal of these collections before purchase is suggested, since many of them are filled with obscure, unusable songs.

The so-called fake books that are used by musicians who play casual engagements are yet another source of material. These consist of lists of tunes placed in alphabetical order and categorized in various ways, such as: musical comedy tunes, swing tunes, and college songs. The lists also provide the key in which each tune is published, together with the starting note. They are handy reference guides. One such booklet is the *Standard Dance Music Guide.* It may be purchased at the Music Exchange, 1619 Broadway, New York, N.Y. 10019.

KEEP A LOOSE-LEAF MUSIC BOOK

As you gradually accumulate an amount of sheet music, categorize the numbers in terms of types, following the order of your notebook. Punch holes in the individual pages and make a music book that will contain all the pieces in your repertoire. Put the pages back to back so that your accompanist will have a minimum of page turns. Also, scotch-tape the outside edges of the sheets.

Some singers cover each page with a transparent plastic in order to protect the pages against damage or pencil markings. If you do this, make sure the plastic you use is nonreflective. The glossy kind of plastic makes it very difficult to read the notes if the light source hits the page the wrong way.

YOUR BEST SOURCE

Listening is your best way of finding new material. Whenever you hear a song on the radio or television that catches your interest, jot down the title and the performing artist. Keep a page of your notebook for such entries. If upon buying the piece and practicing it you find that you cannot use it, remember that a certain amount of trial and error (and wasted money) is to be expected.

Perhaps you have heard a recording of a song that you like very much, but you find that the music is unpublished or out of print. The solution is to find a keen-eared musician who can notate the song from the record and write out a manuscript part for you. However, to make a complete piano-vocal part in this manner can be expensive. A compromise solution that would be less time consuming for the transcriber is to copy only the melody of the song, together with the proper chord symbols. Unless the piece is very complex, such a copy would serve your needs in most cases.

The most common-sense way of acquiring new music is to share your material with your fellow performers. While it is true that some singers may jealously guard a particularly favorite number and be reluctant to share it, most are as anxious as you to expand their repertoire and will gladly exchange music.

AUDITIONS

Like the weather, everyone talks and complains about auditions, and no one can do anything about them. Auditions are frightening, painful, frustrating and maddening, but they are unavoidable. Even well-known stars, no matter what great performances they may have given in the past, must audition at times. The perennial test is "What can you do *now, with this* part, with *this* song?"

In a way, auditions are very democratic because they equalize everyone. It is possible for an unknown performer to be cast in a major role, over a seasoned veteran. On the other hand, the performer must prove himself again and again. He never really "arrives." Hence, auditions.

There are so many unknown factors and subjective elements about any particular audition that to try and second-guess them all would be futile. For instance, you cannot possibly know what goes on in the minds of your auditioners or what personal qualities, physical features, and temperament they are looking for. Occasionally, specific requirements are stated in the audition notices. These will usually be brief descriptions such as: "Thirty-ish male executive type with good baritone voice." At other times the auditioners may have only the haziest idea of whom they are looking for. They may be waiting to have some quality revealed in the course of the auditions.

Given this, all a performer can expect is to come out of an audition and be able to say: "Well, I thought that I gave a good audition." However, being able to say that requires very specific preparation. The following are some hints:

- Audition frequently. The more often you expose yourself to the terrors of auditions, the less terrible they will seem. Even if you don't want to be in a particular show, audition for the sake of desensitizing yourself and building up your confidence.

- Be well prepared. As obvious as this may sound, it is not uncommon to see even an experienced performer make a bad showing because of poor preparation. The most common reason for this is a last minute indecision regarding what to sing and doing new material that has not had time to be solidly learned.

- Try to find out as much as you can about the show or club you are auditioning for. In what musical style is the score written? Is it rock, jazz, or conventional musical theater idiom? If you are auditioning for a musical play, inquire about the casting. Are they looking for a ditzy blonde with a belting voice or a sophisticated society girl with a good head voice? Choose your audition material accordingly.

- Be sure that your music is in good shape. It should be written in the proper key. All markings and instructions on it should be clear and unambiguous. If your music is in separate sheets, they should be taped together so that the order of the pages cannot be mixed up.

- Dress sensibly. Be aware of your good and bad physical features and dress accordingly. Don't be bizarre, thinking they'll remember you better.

- Be aware of the light source when you perform, and be sure that you are seen. Auditions often take place on poorly lit stages where shadows can play havoc with your face. Feel that warm spot of light on your face.
- Remember that as long as you are visible to your auditioners, you are performing. Don't walk on stage in an unattractive manner. You are being judged and evaluated from the moment you appear until you are out of sight. Don't allow yourself to lose your poise and energy after your final note.
- *Don't make eye contact with your auditioners* while you are performing. It is an uncomfortable feeling to be performed *at*. It also tells the auditioners that you are more concerned with their response to you than you are with your song. The exception to this rule is if you are doing a presentational type of song that requires you to make direct contact with the audience. For example, *Cabaret*, *See-Saw*, and *Promises, Promises* all have musical numbers that require direct performer-audience communication.
- A final comment. Whatever the outcome of a particular audition, *try not to draw any conclusion from it*. If you don't get the job, it doesn't mean that you are terrible. Conversely, if you *did* get the job it doesn't mean that you are good. An audition—at least no single audition—does not prove anything about your worth. Some of the most celebrated directors in theater have made some of the most celebrated mistakes in casting. On the other hand, there have been performers who have flunked out at auditions time after time, and who have eventually become stars. Clearly, in some cases a performer's talent has been unappreciated for years.

This is not to say that the results of an audition tell you nothing. Often they are valuable learning experiences, and the feedback that you receive can be used constructively. However, the caution expressed here is that it is easy to over-react to the results of an audition to the point where it becomes a destructive force.

The evaluation that you accept for yourself should come from many sources over a period of time. It should come from professionals you respect, peers, teachers, and especially from your audiences. Combined with your self-knowledge and awareness, these give you a composite picture of yourself as a performer that is more realistic than any one audition.

Appendix B: Relaxation

RELAXATION DISCIPLINES

The contemporary world is one of tension and overstimulation. The big city environment where most performers live is particularly stressful and punishing. When we add to this the problems of the performing profession—job insecurity, auditions, competitiveness, and uncertainties about the future—we have a situation that is potentially dangerous to physical and mental well-being.

Faced with these daily pressures, the individual performer urgently needs to find ways and means of reducing stress, for the sake of his personal happiness as well as his professional success.

Today there are a number of effective relaxation techniques that have been tested and proven. Each of them will give good results, provided that they are practiced in the prescribed manner and are done regularly. I consider the practice of some form of relaxation so important that it should be a part of every performer's daily routine.

PROGRESSIVE RELAXATION

This is a relaxation technique developed by Edmund Jacobson that is widely used for unstressing the entire body. It consists of a systematic tensing and relaxing of all the major groups of muscles so that the body becomes progressively more and more relaxed.

Sit comfortably, preferably in an arm chair. Allow yourself to become quite limp, with head drooping and legs sprawled. Gradually close the eyes. Take a few deep breaths and assume a passive state of mind. Take a few minutes doing this.

Close your fists gradually, applying more and more pressure, until they are tightly closed. While doing this, try to keep the rest of your body relaxed. Hold your fists closed tightly for six seconds. Be aware of how your contracted muscles feel. Now relax your fists completely. Notice how your muscles feel in the relaxed state. Stay in the relaxed state for at least ten seconds.

Now apply this alternation of contraction and relaxation to various groups of muscles, each time contracting the muscles for six seconds and relaxing them for ten seconds. As each new set of muscles become involved, the previous set stays relaxed, so that gradually the entire body goes through the process of relaxation. Relax each muscle group in the following way:

- Tense and relax your forearms, your hands remaining relaxed.
- Hunch your shoulders up as high as you can and hold them that way for six seconds. Relax for ten seconds. (Through all this allow your breathing to be uninterrupted.)
- Tense and relax your neck muscles.
- Squeeze your eyes tightly together, then relax them.
- Press your lips together, then relax. (Do not press your teeth together, only your lips.)
- Stick your tongue out as far as it will go, then relax.
- Take a deep breath and hold it for six seconds. Be aware of the contraction of your chest muscles. Relax for ten seconds.
- Arch your back strongly, then relax.
- Contract your stomach muscles, then relax.
- Raise your legs off the floor, contracting your thighs, calves, and feet. Point your toes in the direction of your head. Relax.

This completes the round of muscle groups. Now scan your body for any residual tensions that may still remain and relax those particular muscles. The whole routine should take about twenty minutes. With daily practice, the process accelerates, so that in a few weeks you should be able to go through the round of muscle groups in a few minutes.

RELAXING WHILE MOVING

Perform some simple actions like sitting down, standing up, lifting an object, or opening a door. Observe which muscles are being used. Are all the muscles being used necessary to perform the action? Can you eliminate any useless contractions?

For instance, in getting out of a chair, do you find yourself contracting your stomach muscles? How about the back of your neck? Is it tight as you get out of the chair? Do your stomach and neck muscles actually help you get out of the chair, or are they superfluous efforts?

Analyze various movements and tasks in this way. Become aware of which muscular contractions are necessary to the task and which are unnecessary or even contrary to the performance of the task.

RELAXING WHILE SINGING

Let us now apply this self-examination process to the act of singing.

While in the standing position, sing a slow melody. As you sing, scan your entire body, starting with the top of your head and proceeding down to your toes. Observe carefully which muscles are being used as you are singing. Check out the following.

- Forehead. Is it wrinkled? Relax it.
- Eyes. Are they relaxed or tense, staring? Soften your look and relax the eye muscles.
- Tongue. Is it lying flat and relaxed in the bottom of your mouth, or is it tense? Relax it.
- Back of the throat. Does it feel open and free or tense and constricted? Open and relax it.
- Lips. Relax them.
- Larynx. Is it down and relaxed, or is it up and tight? Let it come down and relax.

- Back of the neck. Tight or loose? Relax.
- Chest and back. Do they move easily and flexibly as you breathe in and out, or is there tightness and rigidity? Ease up and relax.
- Stomach. Are the stomach walls providing firm but not rigid support for the breath? Relax any excessive tightness.
- Legs and feet. Are you standing easily on your legs, letting the ground support you, or are your grabbing and clutching with your toes and tensing your calves and thighs? Eliminate the unnecessary contractions and relax.

For many singers this self-examination will be a startling experience. When one relizes how many unnecessary, even contrary, muscles are being used in the act of singing, it becomes obvious why serious difficulties are encountered. The singer who uses these contrary muscles blocks himself through his own interference with the natural process.

RELAXATION THROUGH MEDITATION

In recent years meditation has become an important addition to the techniques for relaxation available today. Originally a part of the religious practices of Eastern cultures where meditation is used as a means of enhancing spiritual consciousness, it has successfully migrated to the Western world where its chief application has been as a mind-calming practice.

Experiments with meditators have shown that the general effect of meditation is to decrease the rate of respiration, lower the metabolic rate, and increase alpha wave production in the brain. Although these conditions are associated with relaxation and calmness, the mind is not merely tranquilized or slowed down. On the contrary, awareness is usually sharpened and a feeling of being energized is often reported by meditators.

Though there are many forms of meditation, they are similar to each other in the focusing of the attention on a single idea or object. Awareness may be directed to a part of the body, an external object, or a sound. The most commonly used object of meditation in the West is a mantra. This is a word or sound, usually of one or two syllables, which is repeated to oneself. It may be spoken quietly or heard in the mind only. The most commonly used mantras are *ohm, one* and *down*. The mantra serves as a vehicle for attaining a state of quietness.

- Sit comfortably in a quiet place
- Close your eyes and relax your body.
- Become aware of your breathing. Simply pay attention to it.
- Say the mantra to yourself (inaudibly) as you breathe out.
- If distracting thoughts arise and the mantra goes away, allow it to happen and simply go back to the mantra when it reappears.
- Continue to do this for twenty minutes.
- Allow yourself a minute or two to quietly sit without thinking of the mantra, then slowly open the eyes and resume your activities.

It is best to practice meditation twice daily, usually upon arising in the morning, and late in the afternoon before dinner. However, other schedules are possible, although it is not advisable to meditate right after eating or just before retiring.

Other methods aimed at inducing relaxation are autogenic training, biofeedback training, and hypnosis. The effectiveness of all these techniques will vary due to personal propensities and the continuity of effort. The best results will be had with the help of a qualified teacher.

Appendix C: Coping With Anxiety

PERFORMANCE ANXIETIES

Many well-known performers are quoted as saying that a certain amount of tension and nervousness is necessary in order for them to give a good performance. This heightened excitement and revving up of energy in anticipation of the performance can be a very positive quality. By contrast, other performers suffer from anxieties that are so severe and uncomfortable as to constitute a serious problem. When this kind of anxiety is experienced, the muscles are immobilized, memory freezes, and concentration is destroyed. Such anxiety has nothing to do with healthy nervous energy and is totally negative.

The performer who habitually experiences anxieties while performing has certain typical traits:

- He is a perfectionist. One mistake in a performance will destroy his concentration and upset him.

- He has a history of negative self-evaluation and anticipates the worst in himself.
- He imagines the audience to be composed entirely of critics and enemies.

Anxiety is caused by the attitudes one assumes toward the performance situation. These attitudes express themselves in a number of ways.

- A stream of negative self-evaluations go through the mind of the performer.
- These consist mostly of apprehensive thoughts ("Here comes a high note; I bet I'll crack on it"), warnings ("Watch out! Here's where you messed up the last time"), and predicting the audience's response ("I can tell they hate me. That woman yawned,")
- The body responds to these self-comments by bracing itself as if for an imaginary assault. It becomes tight and inflexible, and the performer feels himself losing control.

All these responses have been learned by the performer sometime in his past history. Now they must be unlearned and replaced by responses that are more realistic. The method for alleviating performance anxieties consists of two distinct elements: (1) Inducing the body to become relaxed and free of muscular tension and (2) counterconditioning the mind by programming it to become desensitized to the anxiety-provoking situation. At the same time, the irrational, negative self-evaluations are replaced with rational, positive self-evaluations. This procedure is practiced away from the performance situation.

Optimally, this technique is best learned in small groups led by an experienced facilitator. However, if the individual has a fair amount of self-discipline, progress can be made by following these instructions.

COUNTERCONDITIONING PROCEDURE

Step 1: Follow the instructions for progressive relaxation described in Appendix B. Be sure that you take the proper time with this section, since it is most important that the entire body be quite relaxed before the next step is taken.

Step 2: When the body has been thoroughly relaxed, visualize a situation that is *mildly* anxiety-provoking. For instance, you are rehearsing for a performance that will take place some time in the future.

While quietly sitting in the relaxed state, vividly imagine the anxiety situation in great detail. As you do so, become aware of your body. How are you breathing? Is your breathing being interrupted or becoming more shallow? Try to further relax your body.

Now attend to your thoughts. Are you indulging in any irrational self-evaluations such as: "They probably won't like me," or "I *know* I'm going to forget the lyrics"? Counter these irrational self-evaluations with rational ones such as: "Audiences have liked me in the past, so they'll probably like me now," or "I've rarely forgotten my lyrics, so it's unlikely that I will now."

Be aware of the degree of anxiety that you are experiencing. Relax away any tension that you notice.

Step 3: Repeat Step 2 with only one change. Visualize a situation that is slightly *more* anxiety-provoking than the preceding one, for instance, rehearsing on the day before the performance.

Step 4: Again, repeat Step 2, this time imagining a still more anxiety-provoking situation.

Step 5: Repeat Step 2, visualizing a yet more anxiety-provoking scene. Perhaps it's now the day of the performance, and you are waiting to go on.

Step 6: Repeat Step 2. This time the situation you choose should be the *most* anxiety-provoking for you. In most cases this will be the actual performance or a difficult passage in a particular song. Now the negative self-evaluations will probably be at their most irrational. Some typical ones are: "I should have rehearsed more. I can't remember what comes next"; "My throat feels sore. I wonder if they can tell"; "Why did I decide to wear this dress (suit). I feel ridiculous in it"; "I feel the audience getting restless. I must be terrible."

As before, these self-evaluations will be replaced with more rational ones, such as: "I've rehearsed an adequate amount of time, so there is no reason to suppose that I won't do well"; "I've had sore throats before and been able to sing with good results"; "I've been complimented on this dress (suit) and have been told that I look very attractive in it"; "I'm doing the best I can right now and if the audience is really restless, it can't be helped. I'll still do the best I can."

Let yourself relax still further and be aware of the degree of anxiety you experience during the exercise.

This completes the counterconditioning procedure. It's most important that the sequence of steps be observed and that no shortcuts be taken. The effectiveness of the procedure depends on the gradualness of the increment of anxiety situations, so that there is a step-by-step progression from the least to the most anxiety-producing situations. The preliminary relaxation routine is equally vital and should not be shortened until some skill in relaxing is developed.

The entire routine should be practiced three or four times a week for at least six weeks. Thereafter, follow-up sessions can be practiced in accordance with the effectiveness of the procedure.

FURTHER HINTS
ON ANXIETY REDUCTION

Rehearse Thoroughly: Every detail of your performance should be carefully rehearsed, allowing an extra margin of time and work for nervousness. Give separate attention to the music, the lyrics, the accompaniment, and stage movement. Likewise, check out the clothing you are wearing, your make-up, props, and so forth.

Perform in Public: The majority of performers find that as they accumulate experience and spend more hours performing in public they become more comfortable on stage and their anxieties gradually lessen. Every opportunity should be taken to perform in public, regardless of the nature of the audience.

Be Involved with Your Material: You can only concentrate on one thing at a time. You can either be involved in your work or your audience, but not both. Most of the exercises in this book are concerned with ways and means of involving yourself in your performance.

Self-Awareness: There is another way of reducing anxiety that uses an antithetical approach to that of involvement. When we involve ourselves, we lose ourselves in the object of concentration, thereby also losing self-awareness. On the other hand, when we become truly aware of ourselves, we lose our preoccupation with extraneous matters such as worrying about slips of memory, how we look to the audience, or whether the audience likes or dislikes us.

In this approach, close attention is paid by the performer to the physical experience of performing. Thus, as you perform, notice carefully:

- Your breathing. Observe when you inhale and exhale. Notice the accompanying movements of your chest and abdomen. Mentally say to yourself: "Now I'm breathing in, now I'm breathing out." You will find that you can do this without interfering with the flow of the lyric as you are singing.

- Your voice. Be aware of the physical quality of the sounds you are making. Say to yourself: "Now I'm singing softly, now I'm getting louder, now I'm accenting this note." Say: "Now the pitch is rising, now it's down, now it's staying on one level."

- Contact with the floor. Be aware of how your feet are in contact with the floor. Feel the floor sustaining your weight. Feel the force of gravity pulling on your body. Be aware of how you balance your body in relation to this pull.

- Body sensations. Notice any particular feeling or sensations in the body: a sensation of warmth, of coolness, an itch, a pain, a tightness or looseness of your clothing.

Objections may be raised that the above approach contradicts all the principles of acting—that without emotion and involvement one cannot create a believeable "reality" on stage. I'm not suggesting that self-awareness be used as a regular approach to performance. It is intended as a corrective, temporary aid to help the performer over rough moments when normal techniques fail and anxiety takes over. Its usefulness lies in its ability to bring the performer into the present and not get tangled up in his projections.

However, aside from its utility as a deflector of anxiety, awareness also has a more legitimate function. By focusing the mind on the concrete, the tangible moment, it accomplishes two things. It prevents the performer from evaluating himself as he performs so that he can't make judgments that will interfere with the work at hand. It also releases intuitive, creative forces and allows them to be expressed without hindrance. There are many testimonies by actors, musicians, and athletes describing the experience of having the conscious mind occupied with simple, direct tasks while the unconscious mind engages in the more important work of creativity. One must experience this in order to be convinced, and it will be worth your effort to do some experiementing with self-awareness.

Other Mind Deflections: The same idea can be applied to external objects. Count the number of rows of seats in the theater while you are singing. Count the number of people in each row. Become aware of the patterns in a drape, the design of a piece of furniture, or a patch of peeling paint on a wall. If you are using a microphone, become aware of its shape, how light reflects off of it, and so forth. Any external object can serve as a point of focus. The purpose is to occupy the conscious mind and to prevent negative self-judgements from taking over.

Do Something Physical: A way of defusing anxiety prior to a performance is to let out some physical energy. Just before you go on stage do some brief physical exercise in your dressing room or in the wings, such as running in place, shadow boxing, dancing, or anything that will release energy. You will find that this has a calming effect on the nerves and serves as a warm-up.

Breathing: When there is anxiety, there is invariably an interference with breathing. At the moment of greatest difficulty—a high note, an awkward phrase, an unsure interval—we stop taking in adequate amounts of air, thereby depriving ourselves of the needed support. Such arrested breathing is a fear response and is similar to our reaction to the threat of a physical blow. When we see a blow coming, we hold our breath and steel our muscles, thereby numbing our body against pain. Psychologically, we react in the same manner. Instead of seeing a blow coming, we imagine criticism or disapproval from the audience and hold our breath. The results of this on a performance is disastrous. Just when we need the most awareness and sensitivity, we stop breathing and numb ourselves.

   Thus, attention to breathing should be the first consideration when anxiety is present. The regularity of breathing must be maintained so there is no stoppage.

Be especially careful just before you begin a song, or before a tough passage or tricky interval. Also, if you're about to make an entrance from the wings of a stage or nightclub, check your breathing and body tension.

Relaxation and anxiety are polarities; they cannot be experienced at the same time. If one is in a relaxed state and only those muscles are used that are necessary to the task at hand, anxiety is impossible. Conversely, in a state of anxiety, muscles necessarily become contracted, interfering with mobility and concentration. By consciously relaxing our muscles we reduce anxiety, and by desensitizing our minds to the anxiety-provoking situation we become more relaxed.

Due to the growing knowledge of the effect that our stressful environment has on the individual, there is a concomitant need to find techniques that will counteract stress. As a result, training in the various disciplines that deal with this problem has become more available. Special programs and workshops are now offered by many universities, Y.M.C.A.s, community centers, and churches.

Appendix D:
Breathing Exercises

Exercise 1: Stand. Breathe normally, but keep your attention primarily on the *exhalation.* Now let the head slump forward on the exhalation. Gradually allow the body to bend forward a little with each exhalation until your fingers touch the floor. Stay there a few moments, then come up a little with each *inhalation* until you reach your original position. This exercise helps center your energy.

Exercise 2: Breathe in and exhale on a prolonged, audible, and whispered *ah.* As you do this, watch for tensions in the stomach, back of the neck, jaw, and tongue. Now breathe in and exhale on the sung vowel *ah* in the middle range. Again, observe your body for tensions.

Exercise 3: Lie on your stomach with your arms at your sides and breathe normally. You will find that in this position the chest cannot move forward, and the rib cage will expand in the back. This is desirable for maximum intake of breath.

Exercise 4: Gasp violently. Hold the breath for a few seconds, then exhale with much energy. Do this three or four times. This exercise energizes the body and helps alleviate anxiety.

Exercise 5: Exhale. Do not take a breath. Constrict your chest as much as you can. Make it as narrow and small a possible. Hold it for six seconds, then violently inhale and expand the chest. Hold it for six seconds. Resume normal breathing.

This exercise has the same purpose as the previous one.

Exercise 6: A tried and true method is *yawning*—opening the throat and relaxing the muscles of the throat, neck, tongue and jaw. After yawning, sing and try to maintain the same openness of the throat.

   Sighing audibly has the effect of relaxing the throat.

   Fast *panting* from the diaphragm is a good way to become energized in a hurry. It develops strength and control of the breath. Follow it with a huge gasp of air, as if startled.

Appendix E: Body Posture and Singing

There is hardly an organ in the body as sensitive as the vocal apparatus. The quality of sound that you make with your voice is affected by your general health, emotional state, thoughts, and the climate. It is most certainly affected by your posture.

Good posture is often associated with an upright, rigid bearing—something like a West Point cadet. Bad posture is identified with a slouched back or a retracted head. Actually, the first, although it may look somewhat better to the average person than the second, should not be emulated either.

Another erroneous attitude is that posture is a static state, a kind of mold into which one casts oneself. But good posture is the dynamic balancing of the body so that the body masses are in proper alignment. It is the state in which there is a maximum efficiency of each member of the body and in which there is a minimum of stress. Good posture is the integration of the various parts of the body into a smoothly functioning whole that has grace and mobility.

The chief obstacles to good posture and easy mobility are chronic muscular tensions. Muscles that are in a permanent state of contraction are immobilized. They also have little sensitivity. In many cases, these tensions are so habitual that they seem normal. They derive from early environmental factors such as being urged to walk and stand too soon in infancy, from imitating poor models, and from physical and emotional trauma. The correction of postural problems usually requires professional help. Nonetheless, a developing awareness can be the beginning of correcting some of the faults. Following are some of the most common ones.

THE FEET

The manner in which your feet support your weight has significance in several ways. They are your connection with the earth—your contact points—and bear the weight of your body. They also express the relationship between you and your environment in how you are "grounded." When the weight of the body is unequally distributed over the feet, tensions will inevitably result. These may develop in the calves, legs, thighs, pelvis, or any part of the body. Clawing the ground with the toes is another expression of tension. The feet should be allowed to spread under the weight of the body.

THE KNEES

The knees should never be locked, but slightly flexed. Locking the knees is a way of bracing yourself, as if your were to receive an imaginary blow. In fact, all bracing of the body may be a form of physical or psychological self defense. From the esthetic viewpoint, locked knees cause the performer to appear stiff and graceless.

THE PELVIS

The torso should balance easily and fluidly on the hip bones of the pelvis. When weight is shifted from one leg to another, the transfer should pass smoothly through the hips and torso. Rigidity in the pelvis is a common defect, reflecting inhibitions learned early in childhood. A rigid pelvis gives the body the appearance of being a solid block. Another prevalent defect, that is particularly unsightly is the so-called sway back, in which the buttocks are pulled backward and upward. Working with a good physical therapist can often correct this problem.

The anal sphincter and buttocks are other areas of frequent tension that particularly affect singers because they interfere with proper breathing. To demonstrate this, simply contract the sphincter muscle and notice the effect this has on the breathing and on the voice.

THE STOMACH

Although the act of supporting the breath requires the abdominal wall to be firm, the muscles of the stomach are too often clutched and rigid. Again, this has a detrimental effect on the voice.

THE RIB CAGE

The rib cage is frequently carried too high or is excessively expanded, adversely affecting the voice. It is also unattractive, giving the singer a stilted "stagey" appearance.

SHOULDERS AND NECK

The shoulders and neck respond most readily to anxiety and stress, resulting in hunched-up shoulders and a retracted head and neck, like a turtle retreating into his shell. This reaction is similar to that of bracing the feet and legs; it is an instinctive attempt to protect the most vital and vulnerable part of the body—the head.

For optimum results, the shoulders must be allowed to drop, and the neck must be free of tension so that it can expand to its natural extension.

THE HEAD

Visible signs of tension in the head are:

The furrowed brow
The tense jaw
The frozen smile
The chin jutting outward and upward (which puts an unnatural pressure on the larynx)
Staring eyes caused by excessive contraction of the eye muscles
The tensed tongue

The head should be lightly balanced on the spinal column, and the neck muscles should be free and uncontracted. The tilt of the head in relation to the spine should be slightly upward and forward, with the chin down. All this should be without the slightest trace of rigidity or force.

If you can imagine dangling from a string attached at one end to the ceiling and at the other end to the top of your head, slightly behind the crown, you will understand the correct relationship of the head with the rest of the body. Another way of realizing this relationship is to lightly grab a tuft of hair in the back of the crown of your head and give it a slight upward tug. Let your head and neck freely follow the direction of the upward pull.[1]

THE BASIC
PHYSICAL REQUIREMENTS

The requirements of today's musical theater (nightclubs to a lesser degree) are such that the performer must be in absolutely top-notch physical condition. The days when a singer could merely stand on stage, face the audience, and sing have long gone by. Since the advent of the director-choreographer in musicals and films, all the old performance criteria have been replaced with newer, more demanding ones. Directors such as Bob Fosse, Michael Bennett, and Jerome Robbins look for performers who can

[1]This and other ingenious exercises in body realignment are to be found in Moshe Feldenkrais, *Awareness Through Movement*, pp. 76–79, 109, 115.

sing, dance, and act well, regardless of what their primary training has been. To meet these requirements, the singing actor must develop disciplined work habits and condition his body in a systematic manner. His routine of training should include:

- Dance classes. Most professional performers, be they primarily singers or dancers, take at least two dance classes a week. These are usually ballet and modern dance, jazz and tap dancing being optional.

- Exercise classes. These classes are oriented toward performers, and their purpose is to develop coordination, suppleness, and strength. Where such classes are unavailable, Hatha Yoga is an acceptable substitute, since the criteria are similar.

- If you are fortunate enough to live in a city that has a good teacher in the Feldenkrais or the Alexander Technique method, avail yourself of this training. Both methods teach the realignment of the body to its natural condition, the correct use of the body, the differentiation of the various members in order to develop maximum mobility, and the total integration of movement so that all parts of the body are in harmony with each other.

- A daily routine of exercises at home should become as habitual as brushing

Bibliography

BARLOW, WILFRED. *The Alexander Technique.* New York: Knopf, 1973.

BENSON, HERBERT. *The Relaxation Response.* New York: Avon, 1976.

BROOKS, CHARLES, V. W. *Sensory Awareness.* New York: Viking Press, 1974.

CHEKHOV, MICHAEL. *To the Actor.* New York: Harper & Row, 1953.

CLURMAN, HAROLD. *On Directing.* New York: Collier Books, 1974.

ENGEL, LEHMAN. *Getting Started in the Theater.* New York: Collier Books, 1973.

ENGEL, LEHMAN. *The American Musical Theater.* New York: Macmillan, 1975.

FELDENKRAIS, MOSHE. *Awareness Through Movement.* New York: Harper & Row, 1972.

FENTON, JACK VINTON. *Practical Movement Control.* Boston: Plays, Inc., 1973.

FUNKE, LEWIS, AND BOOTH, JOHN E. *Actors Talk About Acting.* New York: Avon, 1961.

GROTOWSKI, JERZY. *Towards a Poor Theatre.* New York: Simon & Schuster, 1968.

GUTWIRTH, SAMUEL W. *You Can Learn to Relax.* N. Hollywood, Calif.: Wilshire Book Co., 1972.

HAGEN, UTA. *Respect for Acting.* New York: Macmillan, 1973.

LOWEN, ALEXANDER. *Bioenergetics.* New York: Coward, McCann & Geoghegan, 1975.

MAISEL, EDWARD, AND DART, RAYMOND A. *The Alexander Technique.* New York: University Books, 1970.

MARSHALL, MADELEINE. *The Singer's Manual of English Diction.* New York: G. Schirmer, 1953.

PERLS, FREDERICK; HEFFERLINE, RALPH H.; AND GOODMAN, PAUL. *Gestalt Therapy.* New York: Dell, 1951.

MOORE, SONIA. *The Stanislavski System.* New York: Pocket Books, 1967.

PLEASANTS, HENRY. *The Great American Popular Singers.* New York: Simon & Schuster, 1974.

PROGOFF, IRA. *At a Journal Workshop.* New York: Dialogue House Library, 1975.

STANISLAVSKI, CONSTANTIN. *An Actor Prepares.* Theatre Arts Books, 1936.

STEVENS, JOHN O. *Awareness.* New York: Bantam Books, 1971.

SPOLIN, VIOLA, *Improvisation for the Theatre.* Evanston, Ill.: Northwestern University Press, 1963.

WHITE, JOHN, AND FADIMAN, JAMES, *Relax.* The Confucian Press, 1976.

Index

MUSICAL/SONG INDEX

Editor's Note: Musicals appear in italics, song titles are in quotes. Songs from individual shows are indented under the show title.

185

SUBJECT INDEX